GUIDEPOSTS

TO SELF-DIRECTED LEARNING:

EXPERT COMMENTARY
ON ESSENTIAL CONCEPTS

Edited by
Dr. Gary J. Confessore
and Sharon J. Confessore

Foreword by Dr. Allen Tough

ORGANIZATION DESIGN AND DEVELOPMENT, INC.
KING OF PRUSSIA, PA

Prepared for publication by Organization Design and Development, Inc. Printed in the United States of America.

Library of Congress Catalog Card Number: 92-80286

ISBN: 0-925652-14-8

Contents

Foreword

Later in this book, George Spear's chapter describes the early writing on self-directed learning as "a stream of interest that was to become a flood of popular research productivity." Many of us are eager observers of this flood of research and writing, perhaps standing on the shore to gain ideas for our own teaching, perhaps floating along in a canoe to see where the river will take us, perhaps even contributing further thoughts and data to the existing knowledge. Whatever our connection to the ongoing stream of ideas and studies about self-directed learning, we need guideposts in order to find our way.

This book provides executive summaries of 12 of the best established guideposts. In its third chapter it also describes seven more recent guideposts. And this book itself will quickly earn a reputation as a clear, useful, significant beacon to guide all of us through the fascinating flood of facts, theories, mysteries, and implications concerning the adult's intentional efforts to learn and change.

The implications for organizations, human resource development, educational institutions, and our global future are deep and dramatic. As you read the next few pages, you will find Gary Confessore's pithy statement: to put the common human behavior to work for us in our educational systems and in human resource development ". . . the very first step must be to recognize that self-direction in learning is natural and productive." Indeed, although we are usually not self-conscious about it, self-planned learning is in fact a very normal, natural part of our work and our life. Close to 100 surveys of various groups in 10 different countries have confirmed that about 90% of all women and men conduct at least one highly intentional learning project in any given year. Even more impressive, the typical (middle or average) adult learner conducts five distinct projects, averaging 100 hours each. That is a total of 500 hours a year at major learning efforts — about 10 hours a week. About 70% of these learning projects are planned by the learner himself or herself. No wonder Gary Confessore states that self-direction is *natural*.

He also points out that it is *productive*. Definitely. About 75% of all self-directed learning is motivated by the desire to *use* the knowledge and skill. Studies of self-directed learning in organizations have documented the contribution that it makes to management and productivity. And futurists generally agree that we are very unlikely to achieve a positive future unless we make extraordinary efforts to learn and change.

As the stream of new knowledge about self-directed learning continues to flow, what significant questions might be most useful or fascinating for us to explore? Here are a few of my favorites — questions that remain unresolved despite their importance.

1. What anticipated benefits motivate adults to put forth so much effort to learn? Although it is easy to administer checklists or some other simple method of studying this question, I have not yet seen a sophisticated, conceptual framework for understanding it.

2. Why do most of us, when we are teaching, supervising, or parenting, control the student, employee, or child more than is actually effective? Why do most of us ignore the deep implications of self-directed learning research in our actual behavior? In short, why do most of us tend to *over*-control?

3. Exactly how does self-directed learning, by everyone from a new employee to the CEO, foster the goals of an organization?

4. What are the most optimistic scenarios for the future of adult learning, and what are the most likely scenarios?

5. How widespread is self-directed learning about crucial global issues and humanity's future? What are people now learning, and how? What fosters and facilitates this learning, and what do these learners need most over the next 10 years?

6. As I point out in *Crucial Questions about the Future*, there is general agreement on the key priorities on which we must focus if human civilization is to achieve a satisfactory future. How good is the fit between these priorities and the present curriculum in adult education, universities, and the workplace?

7. How can we get people to stop acting in ways that hurt future generations? How can we help people learn to *care* about the people who will be alive during the twenty-first century? How can we all learn — very rapidly — to transcend our immediate, narrow concerns in ways that will produce a positive outcome for the future of human civilization?

Allen Tough
Ontario Institute for Studies in Education
April, 1992

Preface

How is it that some people always seem to be learning more than was intended or supported by our formal instructional institutions? Some seem to learn outside the bounds of the curriculum when they are in school, others seem to continue to learn new things even after they have completed their formal education. Why is that so? Did you ever notice that some people find it hard to learn in settings where the program is prescribed, yet they do just fine when they set (or at least participate in setting) the goals, procedures, and standards of learning projects? Is such behavior just orneriness or is there some fundamental educational force at work that can be turned to the mutual benefit of learners and the organizations invested in their progress? How can educators and human resource professionals better understand these phenomena in order to do a more efficient and productive job of providing for the educational needs of the organizations and people they serve?

These and several related questions are the focus of a growing number of educators and human resource professionals. Most have adopted the term "self-directed learning" as the name of the phenomenon in question. Many believe the promulgation of sound theory and practice related to self-directed learning may well be the key to more meaningful and productive educational experiences throughout the human lifespan.

Our central purpose in producing this book is to bring the full value of the thinking, research, and writings of leaders in the field of self-directed learning, to a broad audience of educators and human resource developers, in a thorough and efficient manner.

Guideposts to Self-Directed Learning is the result of the cooperative efforts of an international Delphi panel of 49 experts in the field of self-directed learning, representing seven countries. That panel formed a very strong consensus on a list of 12 published works they would recommend as a reading list to anyone who wished to become thoroughly familiar with the phenomenon of self-directed learning, its applications, and its theoretical foundations.

The works selected by the Delphi panel were produced by some of the most respected people in the field of adult education and, from an historical perspective, cover a period of 30 years going back to 1961. The present book is designed to move busy educators and human resource developers through an orientation to self-directed learning in a clear and informative manner. For those who wish to delve more deeply into the subject, we recommend that you use this book as a guide to the selection of original works, as you continue your own self-directed study of this field.

Gary J. Confessore
Sharon J. Confessore
Norman, Oklahoma
April, 1992

Acknowledgements

Nearly all research that involves human subjects requires two kinds of support. One of these is the provision of a stimulating and supportive environment in which to work. The other is the dedication of human subjects who are willing to be poked and prodded, physically or intellectually, until they approach the breaking point.

On this note we sincerely thank our sources of both these types of support. In the first instance, we thank Huey Long, Director of the Oklahoma Research Center for Continuing Professional and Higher Education, as well as the members of the Department of Educational Leadership and Policy Studies of the College of Education at The University of Oklahoma, for providing the physical and intellectual support that put this project in motion. In the second instance, we gratefully acknowledge the very substantial efforts of the members of the International Delphi panel who committed several hours each to participate in the research that led to the production of this book.

This project sought the advice of 49 internationally recognized experts in the field of self-directed learning. Twenty-two of these experts had professional and personal obligations that prohibited their participation within the time limitations we imposed. Most who declined to participate indicated disappointment at not being able to do so, and they expressed their support and interest in knowing the eventual outcome of our work. To these 22 we reaffirm our sense of loss at having to proceed without the benefit of their expert advice.

A very substantial debt is acknowledged to the 27 panel members who were able and willing to commit hours of their personal and professional expertise to this project. During the second iteration these panel members were asked to offer their considered, expert response to 634 technical position statements. Most reported investing four to six hours to complete this one iteration alone.

Twelve panel members contributed chapters to this book and each is introduced to the reader at the outset of his or her chapter. We extend a special thanks to them for their effort and understanding as the book took shape. In addition to those who contributed chapters, there are fifteen others who must be cited for their efforts as members of the International Delphi Panel. Therefore, listed by country and in alphabetical order, we gratefully acknowledge the substantial and loyal efforts of the following panel members.

Canada

Dr. D. Randy Garrison, University of Calgary
Dr. Lillian Hill, University of Calgary (Now at Palm Beach Atlanta College, West Palm Beach, Florida)

France

Dr. Philippe Carre, Interface, Etudes and Formation, Paris

Nigeria

Dr. Gbolagade Adekanmbi, University of Ibadan
Dr. Babatunde Adenuga, University of Nigeria

United States of America

Dr. Rosemary Caffarella, University of Northern Colorado
Dr. Lorraine Gerstner, Our Lady of Mercy Medical Center, Bronx, New York
Dr. Paul Guglielmino, Florida Atlantic University
Dr. Michael Langenbach, University of Oklahoma
Roger Manning, University of Texas at Austin
Dr. Helen Mills, University of Georgia
Dr. Robert Nolan, Oklahoma State University
Terrence Redding, University of Oklahoma
Dr. Charlene Sexton, University of Nebraska
Thomas Shindell, University of Texas at Austin

Finally we thank Dr. Allen Tough, of the Ontario Institute for Studies in Education, for his willingness to associate himself with our project, and for the insightful commentary and challenging questions he presented in the Foreword.

Chapter One

An Introduction to the Study of Self-Directed Learning

Gary J. Confessore

Dr. Confessore is a W. K. Kellogg Fellow at The Oklahoma Research Center for Continuing Professional and Higher Education of The University of Oklahoma. Most of his academic career has been spent as a chief academic officer in institutions of higher education. In that context, he has focused his attention on consensus-building processes and on the continuing professional development of faculty and administrative personnel.

This chapter is designed to provide the reader with a brief and rather simplistic introduction to the study of self-directed learning and to provide a general overview of the organization and contents of the book.

What Is Self-Directed Learning and Why Should You Care?

In an effort to focus the reader's attention on fundamental issues in the study of self-directed learning from the very outset of this book, it would seem appropriate to begin with some discussion of definitions, principles, and limitations to which leaders in the field commonly subscribed. However, given the nature and content of this work, I have elected not to do that in any comprehensive way.

The executive summaries, which constitute Chapters Four through Fifteen of this book, come with rather impressive pedigrees. First, they are impressive because the 12 published works selected for inclusion in this book were identified by an international Delphi panel of experts in self-directed learning. Second, they are impressive because the 12 international experts who prepared the executive summaries are, as a group, a veritable "who's who" of the most widely-published and respected researchers in the field.

It is in the shadow of those daunting pedigrees that I have wrestled with words to provide a brief introduction to fundamental issues addressed in the study of self-directed learning. The narrow bridge has been made even narrower because the central issues of the field are the essential "stuff" of what Sharon and I have come to call "the chapters of substance," which follow. I have elected, in the alternative, to give you some reasons for believing that self-directed learning is something you can expect to see in most people and that your role might be described in terms of how best to be prepared to "let" this natural phenomenon occur rather than on how to structure instruction in order to "make" it happen in your organization.

First, consider the natural function of learning in the human species. On December 6, 1991, I was provided with an eloquent example of the fundamental nature of our need to be active learners and how self-directed learning manifests itself in the human experience. That morning, Terry Anderson appeared on national television for his first press conference as a free man after being held hostage in Lebanon for nearly seven years. Before the conference was over, he gave us a clear example of how simple the phenomenon of self-directed learning is and how critical it can be to the human condition.

As the session proceeded, he was asked several questions that in substance probed the issue of how he and his fellow hostages had maintained their sanity in the face of persistent isolation, harsh conditions, and the constant threat of bodily harm or death. He answered one such question by explaining that for one extended period he was in a cell alone. He could see a fellow hostage in a cell across a narrow and dimly-lit hall. In turn, a third hostage could also see the person across the hall but could not see Anderson. The guards had strictly forbidden them to speak. Anderson went on to explain that he could remember some sign language he had learned years earlier and he taught it to the fellow across the hall, who then taught it to the unseen hostage in the cell adjacent to Anderson. As a result of this effort, the three men were able to communicate at will and without being detected by their guards.

In response to a similar question, he explained that he was not always alone and under orders to remain silent. Most of the time he was with one or two others and free to speak with them. To overcome the long sameness of imprisonment, they taught each other whatever they could. Anderson reported that he had learned something about genetics, statistics, camel breeding, and agricultural economics from his fellow hostages. He explained that he had even spent hours designing a farm, which he could work for profit, if he were ever set free. Then he said something stunningly simple about the role of informal learning projects in the human condition. Referring to the necessity to learn from one another, he said of his fellow hostages, "I needed them. I needed their minds. I needed what they knew."

Anderson's description of how he and the other hostages had organized themselves to learn whatever they valued, setting their own standards and using whatever resources they had access to, speaks directly to the natural function of the human capacity to learn. Very simply, self-directed learning manifests itself in people who feel a need to learn something. In order to reduce this need or "drive," we need only set about assessing, however inexpertly, our internal resources (the ability to reason, read, or cypher) and assessing, however naively, the availability of external resources (human and material) that might be useful to our effort. Once that is done, self-directed learning, as with any other human endeavor, becomes a matter of drive, initiative, resourcefulness, and persistence to see ourselves through to some level of learning that is personally satisfying. It doesn't matter whether the learner utilizes informal or formal support structures. It doesn't matter whether the learner works alone or with others who have a common interest. What Anderson and the other hostages had done, repeatedly, was engage in self-directed learning projects.

It seems that people of all ages and circumstances have been engaging in self-directed learning as a natural condition of life since at least 1830, when, according to Candy (1992), George Craik published a book "documenting and celebrating the phenomenon of 'self-education'." Certainly, several studies cited in the key literature on self-directed learning, which in this book date back to 1961, lead inexorably to this conclusion. But this is only proof that self-direction in learning exists as a human characteristic in the modern world. In truth, it seems to have been a natural behavior of humankind even as the species has evolved.

For example, paleoanthropologists Donald Johanson and Maitland Edey (1981) allow that some evidence associated with their find of *Australopithecus Afarensis* (they named the fossil, Lucy) could mean she lived some three to four million years ago. Moreover, they are convinced that this species was ancestor to all known Homo types. Cosmides and Tooby, in their chapter, *From Evolution to Behavior: Evolutionary Psychology as the Missing Link* (1987), assert

> The evolutionary function of the human brain is to process information in ways that lead to adaptive behavior . . . (p. 282).

What is important here is that at every turn in human evolution, going back as far as four million years ago, we find a cultural record of humankind learning to modify the environment by way of chipping stones, sharpening sticks, making clothing, and so on through the planting of crops, the domestication of animals, and the building of shelters.

For all but the briefest moment of recent human history, all this learning occurred in each generation in the absence of formal, educational structures. Hence, I would submit that the tendency to initiate learning and to use that learning to modify (ostensibly improve) the human condition is not just a characteristic of the species; it is *the* characteristic that defines the species.

How then can we put this natural, and perhaps preferred, human behavior to work for us in our educational systems and in human resource development? I would assert that the very first step must be to recognize that self-direction in learning is natural and productive. In historical terms humankind has spent the overwhelming majority of time depending on informal, or at least extrainstitutional, opportunities to learn about and modify the environment. There is cultural evidence following a direct and unmistakable line from the time humankind first stood erect to the time Terry Anderson made his comments that demonstrate that, left to their own devices, people use their ability to learn to satisfy their own needs.

We must also stop to realize that it is a relatively recent condition of human existence in which we have created a complex network of special places and approved models through which learning is supposed to be stimulated. Formal schools and schooling appeared on the scene only a few thousand years ago. Yet, today we find it very hard to value what is learned outside the formal educational system. As with so many other human-made products, we have come to have greater respect for synthetic substitutes than we have for what nature has provided.

Further, a great many researchers who have asked about how people learn, have found that even with our current cultural preference for formal education, humans of all ages and circumstance regularly engage in learning projects of their own design and for their own purposes. Yet, as a society, we either grossly undervalue such learning or we think of the "self-taught" person as having been involved in some quaint, inefficient, and impractical exercise or even as a person who is acting out some hostility toward our formal (read that "real") system of education.

In order to maximize our efforts to continue to improve the human condition, in the face of growing populations and shrinking natural resources, we must make optimal use of all our human capacities.

That includes those that can be developed through structured, institutional experiences. But it also demands that we use our natural capacities to our greatest advantage. The fact is, we have an enormous and untapped pool of human learning resourcefulness in this tendency of people to organize their own learning projects. As educators and human resource developers, we could conceivably save huge sums of money and uncountable hours of off-line time if we were to tap even the surface of this resource. What is more, this says nothing about the increased productivity that is sure to come from encouraging people to learn what they want, when they want, where they want, and for their own reasons.

Still, consumers and employers have every right to ask whether what we choose to learn on our own meets some minimal standards of relevance, usefulness, and reliability. It is this concern that seems to have led our society to rely on formal curricula and approved credentials, and has simultaneously drawn us away from one of the most powerful learning mechanisms known to humankind, self-direction.

The nature of self-directed learning, how it can be defined, understood, encouraged, and put to productive use in our society and in the workplace, are all topics that are addressed by the works that have been summarized in Chapters Four through Fifteen of this book.

How this Book Is Organized

The present work includes three introductory chapters. After this first chapter of general introduction, you will find a chapter designed to provide an overview of self-directed learning in the workplace. Sections of this chapter address the need for and advantages of self-directed learning from a human resource development perspective. Chapter Three gives a detailed account of how we arrived at the list of works to be covered in this book and how we selected the list of chapter authors. This chapter is included primarily for those who have an interest in the scholarship represented by this effort. However, it is also our sincere hope that it will inspire confidence that the content of this book truly represents the best introductory reading on the topic of self-directed learning to be found under a single cover, in the consensus view of the leading experts in the field.

The "chapters of substance," Chapter Four through Chapter Fifteen, are arranged chronologically in order to give a clearer, historical perspective of the ways in which the several works relate to one another. Hence, Chapters Four through Eight cover the contributions of Cyril Houle's *The Inquiring Mind: A Study of the Adults Who Continue to Learn;* Malcolm Knowles' *Self-Directed Learning: A Guide for Learners and Teachers;* and Allen Tough's *Major Learning Efforts: Recent Research and Future Directions; The Adult's Learning Projects: A Fresh Approach to Theory and Practice in Adult Learning,* 2nd Edition, and; *Learning Without a Teacher: A Study of Tasks and Assistance During Adult Self-Teaching Projects.* These works were published over the period 1961 to 1981. The second set of four chapters covers the contributions of George Spear's and Donald Mocker's *The Organizing Circumstance: Environmental Determinants in Self-Directed Learning;* Stephen Brookfield's *Self-Directed Learning: From Theory to Practice* and *Understanding and Facilitating Adult Learning;* and Rosemary Caffarella's and Judith O'Donnell's *Self-Directed Learning: A Critical Paradigm Revisited.* These works were published over the period 1984 to 1987. The final set of three chapters covers the early contributions of Huey Long and his associates and includes *Self-Directed Learning: Application and Theory; Self-Directed Learning: Emerging Theory and Practice;* and *Advances in Research and Practice in Self-Directed Learning.* These works were published over the period 1988 to 1990. This last set of publications brings to the literature a particular richness and breadth because it is composed of three volumes containing a total of 46 discursive and research-based contributions on the most recent developments in the field of self-directed learning.

References

Anderson, Terry. (1991). Remarks made during an international press conference on the occasion of his release after nearly seven years as a hostage.

Candy, P. C. (1992). Candy on Houle's The inquiring mind: A study of the adult who continues to learn. In J. Confessore & S. Confessore (Eds.), *Guideposts to self-directed learning.* King of Prussia, PA: Organization Design and Development.

Cosmides, L., & Tooby, J. (1987). From evolution to behavior: Evolutionary psychology as the missing link. In J. Dupre (Ed.), *The latest on the best essays on evolution and optimality.* Cambridge, MA: MIT Press.

Johanson, D. C., & Edey, M. A. (1981). *Lucy, the beginnings of humankind.* NY: Simon and Schuster.

Chapter Two

Self-Directed Learning in the Workplace

Sharon J. Confessore

Ms. Confessore is a W. K. Kellogg Fellow at The Oklahoma Research Center for Continuing Professional and Higher Education of The University of Oklahoma. She has served as a trainer and as Dean of a two-year college in New York City. She is presently in the dissertation stage of a program leading to the Ph.D. in Adult Education with an emphasis in Corporate Training and Development.

The primary purpose of this book is to provide the reader with a brief and simplified overview of the most important literature in the field of self-directed learning. The book was designed so that individuals who are interested in incorporating self-directed learning methods into their training programs can acquaint themselves quickly with the key literature in the area. It is hoped that the summaries in this volume will provide readers with "food for thought" and will cause them to seek out and read for themselves those works that seem best to meet their training needs.

Overview

Self-directed learning is not a new concept. Cyril Houle (1961) first popularized the term when he described a study of adults who had engaged in learning activities without support or assistance. This line of inquiry was carried further by his student Allen Tough (1967), who also investigated incidents of adult learning where the entire activity was conceived of, designed, implemented, and evaluated by the individual pursuing the information. Referring to these as "adult learning projects," Tough determined that a broad range of learning activities are self-initiated and self-pursued and that adults are not only very willing but are more than capable of engaging in learning activities without external help.

Self-direction in the corporate setting is usually linked to work teams. In this case, self-directedness refers to activities of semiautonomous groups of individuals within a company who are given responsibility to seek out information, identify possible solutions, and finally implement an appropriate course of action. Self-directed training may be more broadly defined to include all types of training activities, but it specifically refers to the situation where an employee perceives a need for information, identifies an appropriate learning resource, and undertakes an activity that allows the learning (or training) to take place.

Self-directed learning has many advantages. It is an effective method of meeting the challenge of providing timely training in the face of increasing technological requirements. Self-directed learning allows employees to keep current, with minimal time taken for formal training activities. The trend of the 1990's is toward empowered employees, and the nature of self-directed learning encourages employees to build commitment to the training activities in which they become involved. Self-directed learning allows the employee the opportunity to identify individual training needs and to select the most appropriate method of accomplishing the training. This, understandably, increases the commitment of the trainee. Unlike traditional training programs where the employee "shows up" to be taught, self-directed learning makes the employee a partner in the training and learning process, thus stimulating active involvement. Finally, custom-designed programs, developed so that the trainee is able to identify specific goals and training methodologies, encourage commitment to the training sessions.

The Need for Self-Directed Training

A recent report from the U.S. Department of Labor (1991) cites the globalization of commerce and industry and the explosive growth of technology on the job as the two conditions that have changed the "world of work." The report also notes that students are not being prepared adequately for this new world, and because current workers have not been prepared, the United States is playing a catch-up game in the global economy. This is not news to corporate trainers. Effective, efficient training has become more critical than ever for maintaining competitiveness. Today's trainers must constantly balance training delivery methods in order to maintain high productivity against the need of the organization for all employees to be fully engaged in their jobs. Use of self-directed learning may help resolve much of this conflict.

Advantages of Self-Directed Learning

Workers do not need to go through complex, comprehensive programs to use self-directing methods. Self-directed learning in the workplace occurs every day when one worker asks another how to complete a task. Self-directed learning can be formalized and incorporated into the entire workforce by providing people with a support system and by encouraging an environment that makes it acceptable for individuals to ask questions, to search out information, and to develop projects that help the individual obtain the information sought.

The training department can play a key role in the development of a self-directed working environment. Initially, the training department can assist by providing information and by using self-directed training methods in formalized training sessions. To stimulate self-direction in training, the training department might provide seminars to help workers identify areas that are appropriate to self-directed learning. It may also serve as a resource center. In this instance resource center connotes providing all employees easy access to both written and computer managed information as well as a list of individuals in the company and a description of their expertise. The training area thus becomes a center for information exchange.

Self-directed learning can also be tied to an employee's performance appraisal. As companies move toward cooperative work evaluations, the capacity to identify training needs and set up personal learning programs as an integral part of this process provides opportunities to develop clear areas for improvement and specific strategies for accomplishing selected goals. The employee and manager can identify appropriate learning activities and resources for acquiring new information or skills. Conditions for evaluating performance can be specified as part of the learning contract and can be easily evaluated at the end of the performance appraisal period.

With the increased use of self-managed work teams, the appropriateness of self-directed learning becomes obvious. While work teams are organized with particular attention to ensuring that various competencies are present, there are also areas that need to be investigated and studied. Self-directed learning allows team members the opportunity to determine the learning needs of the group and provides a way of obtaining the information the team needs to complete the task assigned. The team can meet to develop a learning project for the group and assign each member a part of the project, or team members can design individual learning projects, with input from other members of the team.

Summary

The role of training in corporations in the United States is changing. As flattening organizations, global competition, and fast-paced technological development become the norm, it is obvious that the training methods of the past will no longer be effective. In their discussion of meeting the challenges of technological change, Rosow & Zager (1988) cite the unending search for a competitive edge; the need for sustained, high-level quality of products; and the need for flexibility and interchangeability of skills in the workforce, as several prime reasons for altering training methods and delivery systems. Peters (1987) recommends that training become a central part of any organization's strategic plan and that continuous learning become an accepted part of the culture of all organizations.

"Continuous learning addresses the threat of obsolescence through a forward-looking, in-service educational policy, which supports the concept of learning rather than the force feeding of training" (Rosow & Zager, 1988). The characteristics inherent in the continuous-learning organization include an overall acceptance of learning as a part of every job; a workforce that is willing and able to learn many jobs and is able to respond to the needs of the organization; and an environment where there is ample interaction among employees so that information is transmitted across lines as well as up and down the organization. Use of self-directed learning strategies promises to be very helpful in developing these characteristics in employees and an invaluable tool for building the appropriate environment necessary for a continuously learning company.

References

Houle, C. O. (1961). *The inquiring mind.* Madison, WI: The University of Wisconsin Press.

Peters, T. (1987). *Thriving on chaos.* NY: Alfred A. Knopf.

Rosow, J., & Zager, R. (1988). *Training: The competitive edge.* San Francisco, CA: Jossey-Bass.

The Secretary's Commission on Achieving Necessary Skills, US Department of Labor. (1991). *What work requires of schools: A SCANS report for America 2000.*

Tough, A. M. (1967). *Learners without teachers.* Toronto, Ontario: The Ontario Institute for Studies in Education.

Chapter Three

Selecting the Key Literature in Self-Directed Learning

Gary J. Confessore and Sharon J. Confessore*

During the fall of 1989 our responsibilities at the Oklahoma Research Center for Continuing Professional and Higher Education placed us in direct communication with the committee that was planning the Fourth International Symposium on Adult Self-Directed Learning, which was to be held in January of 1990. As proposals for papers to be presented at the symposium arrived at the Center, it became apparent that many authors proceeded from an assumption of conflict, or at least an absence of consensus, regarding concepts and issues that would seem to be at the very heart of the study of self-directed learning. In response, the symposium organizers instituted think-tank sessions on theory and application. In part, this was done in an effort to focus the attention of active researchers in the field on the nature and role of these assumptions and on how they may influence our understanding of self-directed learning.

The think-tank sessions held at the symposium were well attended and they generated animated discussions that yielded only limited agreement on critical issues. Thus, Long (1991) was moved to note, "self-directed learning as a theoretical, research, and applied topic may be compared to a gangling adolescent whose physical growth has not been matched by social, emotional, and mental maturity" (p. 2).

The manuscripts selected for inclusion as chapters in the book published subsequent to the Fourth International Symposium on Adult Self-Directed Learning, and the think-tank reports from that symposium, clearly emphasized the extent to which philosophical,

---

*This chapter is an adaptation of Confessore, Gary J. & Confessore, Sharon J. (1992). In H. B. Long & Associates. *Self-directed learning: Research and application.* Norman, OK: Oklahoma Research Center for Continuing Professional and Higher Education.

methodological, operational, and personality conflicts dominate discourse in the field. Indeed, this pattern was so clear that the 1991 book by Long and Associates was titled, *Self-Directed Learning: Consensus and Conflict.*

Moreover, where consensus emerged in the think-tank sessions, it did so in a diffuse and tentative way. As active participants in both the theory and application think-tank sessions, we were left with the sense that perceived conflicts grew more out of limitations of time and process that forestalled emergence of consensus than out of actual disagreement. That is to say, it seemed the activity was too brief and the process did not allow for full consideration of a broad range of ideas in a non-confrontational setting. Hence, no individual or group of individuals had sufficient opportunity to stimulate the formation of consensus around critical issues in the field.

At the close of that symposium, we determined to undertake a comprehensive effort to discover the extent to which consensus regarding the recent accomplishments and near future objectives of the field might be formed. Properly structured, such an effort might help researchers distinguish between areas where there is true conflict and areas where existing consensus has not been reported as such.

Methodology

The Delphi technique was developed by Norman Dalkey and Olaf Helmer (1963) for use by the Rand Institute in the early 1950's. Basically, the process is designed to provide a non-confrontational environment in which diverse views on a topic may be elicited and receive thorough consideration on the extent to which others agree or disagree with those views. This process is often used to arrive at consensus on issues that cannot be settled empirically, such as predicting future events. In other cases it has been used to form a consensus as to the relative merit or importance of attitudes, assumptions, or research findings.

In order to use the Delphi technique, a panel of "reputational experts" must be selected. These "experts" may share specific experiences, skills, knowledge, or membership in a community of common concern. Once the panel is impounded, the members participate in a paper exercise in which their contributions and responses to the contributions of others are never identified by source to anyone but the research managers. In the first iteration, panelists are asked to respond to open-ended questions. Their answers are then compiled, without editing, into a single report using a code system, such as identification numbers. This allows panelists to track their own contributions while

masking the source of items contributed by others. In the second iteration, the panelists are asked to indicate the degree to which they agree
or disagree with each contribution, using a Likert-type scale. These
responses are analyzed to discover which, if any, have elicited a
response pattern that represents a statistically significant consensus.

In the study that led to this book, response patterns were subjected to analysis using the Kolmogorov-Smirnov One Sample Test
(Siegel, 1956) to determine whether the actual cumulative distribution of responses to each item deviated significantly from a theoretical cumulative distribution. The result of this calculation is referred
to as the value of "D." In the second iteration, items were differentiated according to whether they had attracted a simple majority of the
panel indicating agreement or disagreement.

In the third iteration, each panelist received individually structured survey forms that asked for responses to only those items for
which his or her second iteration response fell outside the emerging
consensus. Sufficient information was given to inform each panelist
of the magnitude, direction, and distribution of the emerging consensus, and a record of his or her outlying response was provided.
Panelists were asked to review their second iteration response in light
of the emerging consensus. If they wished to change their response,
they were welcomed to do so. In the alternative, if they wished to
provide an explanation of their reasons for remaining an outlyer, that
information would be of value in understanding the limits of the
emerging consensus.

Finally, the Kolmogorov-Smirnov was used again to determine the
significance of the response patterns. Additionally, in this final iteration, only those items whose volume of agreement was at least one
standard deviation above the mean for responses found to have a statistically significant response pattern were retained in the consensus.

The Delphi Panel

Because this study was motivated by observations made at the
Fourth International Symposium on Adult Self-Directed Learning, it
was decided that the Delphi panel should be composed of individuals
who had some formal connection with one or more of the four
annual, international symposia on adult self-directed learning. An
effort was made to balance the panel according to important philosophical and methodological issues by including quantitative and
qualitative researchers, some of whom believe the field is on the right
track, some who have expressed substantial concern that the field is
an important distraction to adult educators, and others who have

recanted their earlier substantial involvement in the field. Application of these criteria yielded a list of 49 possible panelists representing seven countries. For purposes of this study, these individuals were designated "reputational experts."

These reputational experts were provided an outline of our research objectives and of the Delphi process. They were then asked to respond to 10 open-ended questions regarding their judgment about selected issues in self-directed learning. Consensus was sought on the following items:

1. In your judgment, what are the three most important research findings that have been reported to date in the literature on adult self-directed learning?

2. In your judgment, what are the three most important trends in research into adult self-directed learning?

3. Please list the three most important changes in educational *theory* that, in your judgment, are attributable to research into adult self-directed learning.

4. Please list the three most important changes in educational *practice* that, in your judgment, are attributable to research into adult self-directed learning.

5. Please provide the citations for the three most important published works that, in your judgment, should be read at the outset of one's introduction to the field of adult self-directed learning.

6. Please list the three most important issues in adult education that, in your judgment, should be researched between now and the year 2000.

7. Please list the three most important changes in educational *theory* during the 1990's that will, in your judgment, be precipitated by research into adult self-directed learning.

8. Please list the three most important changes in educational *practice* during the 1990's that will, in your judgment, be precipitated by research into adult self-directed learning.

9. Please list the three most important sources that, in your judgment, will produce researchers in the field of adult self-directed learning during the 1990's.

10. Please list the three most important questions not included above that, in your judgment, should be asked in future surveys.

A detailed report of the findings of this survey are reported in Confessore & Confessore (1992). However, for our purposes in this book, we shall focus only on the responses to item five for which we sought the panel's advice in compiling a list of the "most important published works . . . in the field of self-directed learning."

Quantitative Findings

Twenty-seven panelists representing five countries elected to participate in the study and returned completed, first iteration response forms. Figure 3.1 reveals the rate at which a general consensus emerged on the issue of important published works. Note that the number of "possible" responses to this survey was set at 81. This reflects the fact that 27 panelists agreed to provide up to three responses to the target question. The number of citations obtained in the first iteration was 34, or 41.98% of the diversity possible, assuming there had been no agreement whatever across the panel.

In the second iteration, 23 panelists returned completed surveys. Fifteen of the 34 citations, or 18.52% of the possible diversity, attracted a simple majority agreement, the pattern of which was not likely to be a chance distribution.

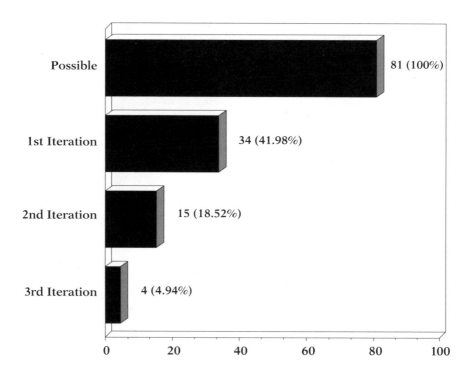

Figure 3.1 Emergence of Consensus Over Three Delphi Iterations.

In the third iteration, 22 panelists returned completed surveys. Four of the original 34 citations, or 4.94% of the possible diversity, had response patterns that were not likely to be a chance distribution, *and* the volume of agreement with these items was at least one standard deviation above the mean volume of agreement for all citations.

The volume of responses to survey items in the first iteration provides a general impression of the relative diversity of opinion at the beginning of the Delphi process. For example, of the 10 items in the original survey, the item on important published works drew citations amounting to only 41.98% of the diversity possible (31 of 81). It is important to note that initial diversity of response does not necessarily equate directly to lack of agreement. For example, item six of the original survey drew 76 of a possible 81 responses, or 93.83% of the diversity possible. Yet, in the final iteration, the panel had reached consensus on 17 of those responses. This represents the greatest breadth of agreement for all items in the survey.

In order to arrive at a list of recommended readings on which there is substantial expert agreement, we expanded our consideration to include those citations that had attracted majority support and for which the panel's response pattern was not attributable to chance. The list of recommended readings grew to 12. It is those 12 citations that we have designated as the key literature and that have been summarized in this book. They are listed below in the order of the strength of consensus that was built over three iterations.

These are the citations for the most important published works that, in the panel's judgment, should be read at the outset of one's introduction to the field of adult self-directed learning. Each citation is preceded by the number of the final 22 panel members who joined the consensus and the degree of statistical significance calculated for the item. For example, Tough's 1979 book attracted a unanimous decision for which the chances were less than one in one hundred that the response pattern represented a chance distribution. His 1981 book attracted a simple majority of 12 out of 22 in a response pattern for which the chances were less than five in one hundred that the response pattern represented a chance distribution.

1. 22 .01 Tough, A. (1979). *The adult's learning projects* (2nd ed.). Toronto, Ontario: Ontario Institute for Studies in Education.

2. 20 .01 Houle, C. O. (1961). *The inquiring mind* (2nd ed.). Madison, WI: The University of Wisconsin Press.

3. 20 .01 Long H. B. & Associates. (1988). *Self-directed learning: Application and theory*. Athens, GA: University of Georgia, Department of Adult Education.

4.   19 .01   Brookfield, S. D. (1985). *Self-directed learning: From theory to practice.* (New Directions for Continuing Education, No. 25.) San Francisco, CA: Jossey-Bass.

5.   18 .01   Knowles, M. (1975). *Self-directed learning: A guide for learners and teachers.* Chicago, IL: Follett.

6.   18 .01   Long, H. B. & Associates. (1989). *Self-directed learning: Emerging theory and practice.* Norman, OK: Oklahoma Research Center for Continuing Professional and Higher Education.

7.   17 .05   Spear, G. E., & Mocker, D. W. (1984). The organizing circumstance: Environmental determinants in self-directed learning. *Adult Education Quarterly, 35*(1), 1-10.

8.   17 .05   Tough, A. (1978). Major learning efforts: Recent research and future directions. *Adult Education Quarterly, 28*(4), 250-63.

9.   15 .05   Long, H. B. & Associates. (1990). *Advances in research and practice in self-directed learning.* Norman, OK: Oklahoma Research Center for Continuing Professional and Higher Education.

10.   13 .05   Brookfield, S. (1986). *Understanding and facilitating adult learning.* San Francisco, CA: Jossey-Bass.

11.   13 .05   Caffarella, R. S., & O'Donnell, J. M. (1987). Self-directed adult learning: A critical paradigm revisited. *Adult Education Quarterly, 37*(4), 199-211.

12.   12 .05   Tough, A. (1981). *Learning without a teacher: A study of tasks and assistance during adult self-teaching projects.* Toronto, Ontario: Ontario Institute for Studies in Education.

Selection of Chapter Authors

Each of the following chapters was written by a member of the Delphi panel. Because each of the panelists is a "reputational expert" of international stature, we could have asked any one of the panelists to write the executive summary of any one of the works selected by the process. However, we felt there was a strong rationale to support the position that each work would best be summarized by one of the panelists who had originally nominated the work during the first iteration. Beyond seeming to be fundamentally fair, this solution carries with it the added advantage of a strong advocacy for the work.

Conclusion

The study that led to this book found that among leaders in the field of self-directed learning, there is substantial breadth and depth related to 10 central issues. Yet this consensus is limited temporally and in terms of content. The Delphi technique has proven to be effective in allowing this consensus to emerge among these panelists, on these issues, at this time. The single issue of determining what published works should be read as an introduction to the field will, happily, never be settled for long. As new works are published, the reading list will have to be reviewed. As this work goes to press, we would like to bring several recent books to your attention. Because they had not seen the light of day when the Delphi panel was surveyed, they could not be assessed relative to other works in the field. Indeed, no such assessment is implied by their inclusion here. Yet, because of the importance of the previous contributions of these authors, we believe you should at least be aware of the availability of their most recent books. We recommend you consider adding the following recent publications to your reading list:

1. Brockett, R. G., & Hiemstra, R. (1991). *Self-direction in adult learning: Perspectives on theory, research and practice.* NY: Routledge.

This book synthesizes developments, issues, and practices in self-directed learning. It (1) introduces self-direction as a way of life by presenting three adult learners' stories, (2) provides a conceptual framework for understanding self-direction and summarizes the underlying knowledge base for self-directed learning, (3) focuses on research related to adults' learning projects, (4) centers on the SDLRS and OCLI, two quantitative instruments related to self-directed learning, (5) describes qualitative efforts used to understand the topic, (6) describes how self-directed learning can be facilitated, (7) provides strategies for enhancing learner self-direction, (8) focuses on institutional perspectives, (9) describes some related policy issues, (10) summarizes self-directed learning in various countries, (11) outlines some ethical dilemmas that exist when instituting self-directed learning, (12) describes what a future family might be like with self-directed learning incorporated into their daily living, and (13) closes with various thoughts and recommendations for the future.

2. Candy, P. (1991). *Self-direction for lifelong learning: A comprehensive guide to theory and practice.* San Francisco, CA: Jossey-Bass.

Based on an extensive review of almost 1,000 items of literature drawn from different research traditions and various countries, this book comprises a major critical analysis and significant reformulation of the theoretical basis of self-directed adult learning. It (1) traces the history of self-directed learning and explores recent factors that have increased its prominence, (2) distinguishes between self-direction as a process and as a product and further distinguishes self-directed learning inside and outside formal instructional settings, (3) brings together much recent applied research and theoretical speculation about learning and provides a new way of understanding self-direction in learning from a constructivist perspective, (4) includes three chapters specifically concerning the development or enhancing of capabilities for self-directed learning and presents a three-part model for facilitating such learning, and (5) concludes with a survey of major traditions in research and offers alternative strategies and directions for future research in the domain.

3. Long, H. B. & Associates. (1991). *Self-directed learning: Consensus and conflict*. Norman, OK: The Oklahoma Research Center for Continuing Professional and Higher Education.

This book examines the challenges that reside in the concepts, definitions, and theoretical dimensions of self-directed learning. Discussion focuses on four topics: (1) a brief, historical overview places the topic in time and identifies scholars who were associated early with adult self-directed learning, (2) conceptual and definitional challenges are noted, (3) theoretical and procedural challenges are discussed, and (4) practice challenges are presented.

Conclusions reached by the chapter authors include the following: (1) There are some questions as to whether self-direction in learning as a goal relates to the learning process or the consequences of the learning activity. (2) Some of the theoretical challenges emerged from some of the early discussions of self-directed learning that failed to distinguish between self-directed learning as a therapeutic, humanistic, psychological activity and educational activity. (3) It is important that the theoretical framework developed for self-directed learning be an interactionist theory that provides for multiple variables. (4) Challenges to practice raise a number of questions for scholars to address, such as: What kinds of learning environments are more conducive to self-directed learning? What kinds of teacher behaviors are most supportive of self-directed learning? What kinds of evaluation procedures are more appropriate and useful to assess the consequences of self-directed learning? How does the teacher develop and/or strengthen attitudes favorable to self-directed learning? How do the kinds of support activities differ according to learning environment? How does recognition for intrinsically motivated learning affect the strength of such motivation? How can teachers employ differential learning conditions for learners with differing levels of self-directed learning?

4. Long, H. B. & Associates. (1992). *Self-directed learning: Research and application.* Norman, OK: The Oklahoma Research Center for Continuing Professional and Higher Education.

This is the most recent in a series of books growing out of the works presented at the annual International Symposium on Self-Directed Learning. Because this book is still in press, we have made no attempt here to provide an abstract of its contributions to the literature.

5. Confessore, G. J., & Long, H. B. (1992). *Abstracts of literature in self-directed learning, 1983-91.* Norman, OK: The Oklahoma Research Center for Continuing Professional and Higher Education.

6. Long, H. B., & Confessore, G. J. (1992). *Abstracts of literature in self-directed learning, 1966-1982.* Norman, OK: The Oklahoma Research Center for Continuing Professional and Higher Education.

7. Long, H. B., & Redding, T. (1991). *Self-directed learning dissertation abstracts, 1966-1990.* Norman, OK: The Oklahoma Research Center for Continuing Professional and Higher Education.

As one might infer from the titles of these last three citations, these books constitute a comprehensive source of information about the body of literature produced in the field of self-directed learning over the period 1966-1991.

References

Confessore, G. J., & Confessore, S. J. (1992). In search of consensus in the study of self-directed learning. In H. B. Long & Associates, *Self-directed learning: Research and application.* Norman, OK: Oklahoma Research Center for Continuing Professional and Higher Education.

Dalkey, N. & Helmer, O. (1963). An experimental application of the Delphi method to the use of experts. *Management Science, 9*(3), 458-77.

Long, H. B. (1991). Self-directed learning: Consensus and conflict. In H. B. Long & Associates, *Self-directed learning: Consensus and conflict* (pp. 1-9). Norman, OK: Oklahoma Research Center for Continuing Professional and Higher Education.

Siegel, S. (1956). *Nonparametric statistics for the behavioral sciences.* NY: McGraw-Hill.

Chapter Four

The Inquiring Mind: A Study of the Adult Who Continues to Learn*

Philip C. Candy on Cyril O. Houle

Dr. Candy is Professor of Adult Education and Director of the Academic Staff Development Unit at Queensland University of Technology. His most recent book, Self-Direction for Lifelong Learning: A Comprehensive Guide to Theory and Practice, *earned the 1991 Cyril O. Houle World Award for Literature in Adult Education published in the English language.*

If you were to survey the literature of adult education from the late 1950s and early 1960s, three features in particular would probably strike you. The first is the relatively small amount of literature that was available to scholars and practitioners at that time. The second is that the literature was dominated almost exclusively by sociological concepts, including questions of participation and non-participation and wider issues of the social impact of adult education. The third major difference was that the field, which after all had only really developed as an area of scholarly inquiry since the second world war, was even then showing signs of a preoccupation with quantitative methods of research.

It was into that particular situation that Houle's brief book *The Inquiring Mind* was born. Cyril Houle was already a distinguished teacher, scholar, and researcher of adult education at the University of Chicago when, in 1960, he was invited to take up the Knapp

---

*Cyril O. Houle (1961). *The inquiring mind: A study of the adult who continues to learn.* Madison: University of Wisconsin Press (reprinted in facsimile, with a Foreword by H. B. Long and an Afterword by C. O. Houle, 1988, Norman, Oklahoma Research Center for Continuing Professional and Higher Education. Except where otherwise indicated, all page references are to this second edition).

Visiting Professorship at the then newly established Milwaukee Campus of the University of Wisconsin. As Houle writes, "One of the assignments of the Knapp Professor is to deliver a series of public lectures" (p. xi), and it is out of that set of lectures that *The Inquiring Mind* grew.

Houle entered into the requirements of the Knapp Professorship by preparing a lecture series in which he was clearly mindful that "an audience drawn from many disciplines as well as from the general public expects that a speaker will deal with a theme of widespread interest" (p. xii). As a result, he selected a topic which, "though it is at the heart of the specialized field of adult education, should also be a matter of concern to everyone: what kinds of men and women retain alert and inquiring minds throughout the years of their maturity" (p. xii)?

Years after the event, Houle was to confess that, in 1960, he "was like the preacher who has no sermon to give but who has to give a sermon. I had to present a series of lectures — and soon, too — and could undertake only as much investigation as would provide content for them" (p. 90). Perhaps we should be grateful for the constraints imposed by the impending Knapp lectures. Instead of the "detailed, controlled, and lengthy investigations flowing from clear hypotheses and resulting in mature and reasoned theory" (p. 90) that Houle would have preferred, we ended up with this concise, lucid, and forceful set of essays.

It is hard to know whether Houle, in 1960, had a sense of the profound significance that his lectures (and the subsequent publication of *The Inquiring Mind*) would ultimately have on the field of adult education. Writing a foreword for the Second Edition — more than a quarter of a century after the original appearance of the book — Houle claims that the early 1960s was "a time when adult education needed a new major theme to orient scholarly analysis" (p. 89), because "the focus of [the then] current literature was almost entirely on social actions and responses" (p. 89). It is a tribute to Houle that, in the face of "apathy and scorn" (p. 89), he chose to "enlarge the existing discourse [in adult education] by focusing on the learner as well as on the collective learning process" (p. 90).

While it may be an exaggeration to claim that *The Inquiring Mind* singlehandedly turned the tide of research in adult education, it is certain that this brief and elegant book — both methodologically and in terms of its content — did mark a major break with previous research and represented a significant milestone in the development of the field.

Background to the Book

To obtain the data for his lectures and for the book that grew out of them, Houle interviewed 22 continuing learners — people who were recommended to him as avid adult learners, all of whom lived within a 75 mile radius of Chicago. He interviewed each of them at length, probing them to find out about their backgrounds and upbringing, their life experiences, their interests, and their attitudes toward education, especially self-education. He tape recorded each interview and used transcripts of the interviews as the basis for preparing the lectures.

In doing these interviews, Houle broke new ground; first by moving away from the prevailing notion that research always had to involve large numbers of respondents and preferably a lot of statistics; and second by placing the learners themselves and their personal values and aspirations at the center of the research process. While neither of these things seems particularly revolutionary now, it must be borne in mind that both these emphases were considered highly unorthodox 30 or more years ago.

In a five-page Note on Method, which forms a supplement to the main text, Houle explains that he sent out a two-page background statement to those people who agreed to be interviewed, explaining both the purpose and the process of the study. He also mentions that in the interviews themselves he used "a series of nineteen major questions with a number of subquestions designed to get at the following points:

1. Do continuing learners possess any particular characteristics that make them different from other people?
2. What were the factors that led them to become continuing learners?
3. What has been the history of their continuing education in the past?
4. How much education are they now undertaking and of what kinds?
5. How do they think society views continuing education?
6. How do they themselves view it" (p. 83)?

As a result of these interviews, Houle did two major things: first, he developed a typology of reasons for participating in adult education activities; and second, he placed the self-educational efforts of adult learners into the explanatory context afforded by this typology.

In doing this, Houle effectively sparked two strands of research in adult education, which today we recognize as "participation" and "self-directed learning." Although these domains have since diverged and each has spawned its own considerable literature, it is worth considering the impact they had on each other when they are traced back to their shared headwaters.

Based only on the content of his interviews he writes, "I had no conscious hypotheses" (p. 14). Houle identified three motives that cause people to participate in educational activities. These he labelled goal oriented — "those who use education as a means of accomplishing fairly clear-cut objectives" (p. 15); learning oriented — "those who seek knowledge for its own sake" (p. 16); and activity oriented — "those who take part because they find in the circumstances of the learning a meaning which has no necessary connection . . . with the announced purpose of the activity" (p. 16).

It is worth noting in passing that, despite his encyclopaedic knowledge of earlier literature on adult learning, Houle was apparently unaware that a very similar typology had been advanced almost a century earlier. In 1864, Charles Knight, a well-known London publisher and influential member of the Society for the Diffusion of Useful Knowledge, had produced his memoirs in which he discussed the origins of a book he had published in 1830 by George Craik, documenting and celebrating the phenomenon of self-education. He wrote:

> In the preliminary stages of discussion on the objects and mode of treatment of a book such as this, which was to embrace a vast number of illustrative anecdotes of the love of knowledge overcoming the opposition of circumstances, there were necessarily different estimates of the value of scientific and literary studies, whether "for use," or "for delight," or "for ornament" (1864, Vol. II, p. 133).

While in no way diminishing the significance or the originality of Houle's contribution to our literature, it is instructive to recognize that even pioneering works such as *The Inquiring Mind* have an intellectual ancestry. The three categories of motives — goal oriented, learning oriented, and activity oriented — are remarkably similar to Knight's three "values of scientific and literary studies" — for use, for delight, and for ornament — respectively.

The Book Itself

Many of the publications on self-direction that are discussed elsewhere in this book are relatively long and, in at least several cases, are rendered difficult to review because they are edited volumes with a diverse range of contents and perspectives. Houle's book, however, is neither of these. Crisp and succinct, it is the earliest and arguably the briefest book specifically on adult self-directed learning and is unwavering in its attempt to explore the world of adult learning from the learner's point of view. Aside from a three page Preface in which Houle explains the genesis of the Knapp Lectures, and a five-page Note on Method at the end, *The Inquiring Mind* comprises just 82 pages of text, divided into three chapters of approximately equal length.

The first chapter, titled "Two Educations," begins by addressing the central theme of why some adults choose to participate "to an outstanding degree in activities which are commonly thought to be educational" (p. 4). Whereas previous research had considered what sort of people choose to participate in the programs of particular providers, Houle began with the educational efforts of individuals ". . . not with the act of participation but the participant" (p. 4). It is in this first chapter that Houle advanced his now famous three-part typology of reasons for participating in continuing education, yet he never envisaged them as watertight and mutually exclusive compartments. Toward the end of the chapter, Houle observes of the people interviewed:

> All of the people in the sample are basically similar; they are all continuing learners. They have goals; they enjoy participation; and they like to learn. Their differences are matters of emphasis. Most of them fit clearly into one or another of the three groups but none is completely contained thereby. A few people stand so near the boundary between groups that there might be difference of opinion as to where they should properly be classified (p. 29).

He also points out that whatever the validity of this three-way split as applied to learners, "the grouping [cannot] be extended to educational activities themselves; a particular course, for example, may attract representatives of all three groups, each attending for his [her] own distinctive reason" (pp. 29-30).

The second chapter is titled "Step to the Music," and it begins with a neat analogy between how bats navigate in the dark (by emitting noises whose echoes guide their flight) and how adult educators conventionally plan their offerings by "guiding our courses of action chiefly by what comes back to us as echoes from what we ourselves say" (p. 32). Instead, Houle argues, adult educators ought to base their offerings on the diversity of motives (and self-concepts) that adult learners bring with them to any learning situation. He makes the point again that an individual's motives are seldom monolithic and even less frequently static. Consequently, program planners need to account not only for a diversity of possible motives in their participants but also for changing patterns and coalitions of interest as activities proceed.

Linked to this is the valuable but often ignored insight that, "Those who try to educate adults or who study the best methods of teaching the mature mind are themselves often oriented primarily towards goals, or activity, or learning for its own sake . . ." (p. 52). Like so much else in this book, the assertion that adult educators have conceptions of education that affect their practices has proved to be well ahead of its time. Only in the past few years have researchers turned their attention to the study of teachers' thinking, and more recently to identifying the effects of matches and mismatches between teachers' and learners' expectations — of themselves and of each other.

Another remarkably contemporary note comes right at the end of Chapter Two, where Houle writes:

> What is needed is a more concerted effort, by educators and such allies as they can enlist among the value-establishers of our society, to express the importance of continuing education as clearly and as universally as they can so that the message finally penetrates to all those different clusters and groups of people who make up the public . . . anybody who cares to do so can help by trying to establish or to enlarge an enclave made up of those who support the idea that learning is a natural way of life. Perhaps some day the edges of the expanding enclaves will all meet and there will no longer be any surrounding foreign dominions (p. 54).

This represents as elegant a statement as one could possibly make about the concept of a "learning society," a concept that has really only made its mark in recent years.

The third chapter of *The Inquiring Mind* is titled "A Cataract of Consequences," and its central argument is that whatever motive or combination of motives appears to impel a particular learner to engage in learning, there is no single or simple explanation for their interest. Many adult educators — administrators, policy makers, researchers, and teachers — assume a simple, linear causality between the detection of some need or interest and its realization or fulfillment through involvement in a particular adult education program or activity. This view, argues Houle, is simplistic and misleading. Behind any decision to learn something new (and in particular to enroll in a course or program in order to learn something new) lies a complex network of motives, interests, and values, and behind them, yet another layer of complexly interlinked factors: "a cataract of consequences." Houle writes:

> This effort to explore the reasons why some people become continuing learners has made it clear that there is no simple answer to this complex question. At the end . . . we realize that we must ask 'Whys?' not 'Why?' Probably we shall never get at all the facts, though further research should give much clearer answers. Each person is unique and his [or her] actions spring from a highly individualized and complex interaction of personal and social factors (p. 80).

Idiographic research, based on the purposes, intentions, understandings, and perceptions of individual learners, is only now starting to catch up with the wisdom of this insight.

Implications for Practice

The Inquiring Mind was not written as a manual for program planners nor as a how to recipe book for practicing adult educators. Nevertheless, although it was not intended or envisaged as an applied book, there are still several findings that have important implications for practicing, adult educators, as well as for researchers.

The first, as already discussed, is that in any formal adult education activity (whatever its ostensible focus) there are likely to be some learners whose motivation is primarily goal oriented, some activity oriented and some learning oriented. Not only are these motives mixed within the one group but, as one reviewer commented, ". . . like airline schedules, [they] are subject to change without notice" (Williams, 1963, p. 123). This means that adult educators must be both responsive and flexible: responsive in the sense that they must respond to the learners' motives and interests and, unlike bats, not simply to listen to the echo of their own intentions in putting on the program; and flexible because learners can and do shift their intentions as a program unfolds and develops.

The second major finding, not just for adult educators but in fact for all educators, is that teachers were seldom identified as significant stimulators of people's desire to learn. Librarians were frequently mentioned, and so too were other continuing learners. The implication is that adult educators need to think of themselves as catalysts and facilitators, in particular, putting learners in touch with appropriate resources and assisting them to network with other learners. The social nature of much self-directed learning has often been obscured by an excessive emphasis on individualism, whereas Houle's research points up the vital significance of other people in the learning endeavors of many adults.

Third and finally, Houle identified that, contrary to expectations, the major enemy of continuing learning is "not apathy, as many would like to believe, but outright opposition, and opposition from places where it counts most — from the family, associates, and friends who surround the person who feels an inclination towards learning" (p. 46). Many of those interviewed thought that other people were critical of them for continuing to learn: "They call me the professor or Einstein or something like that"; "They think I'm creepy"; "They say, 'Aren't you ever going to grow up?'"; "They think I'm crazy" (p. 44). In a society that supposedly values self-improvement and places a premium on the benefits of learning, this was a particularly shocking finding. Whether this still applies thirty years later is hard to judge; certainly the rhetoric of both personal and societal advancement through self-education is commonplace today. But Houle's recommendation would still seem to be appropriate: to foster a love of learning and to encourage the emergence and development of supportive enclaves until they expand, overlap, and eventually envelop society. Listen to Houle's powerful clarion call:

> By building a strong and coordinated national program of adult education, we might hope to broaden the spirit of inquiry . . . until it includes all aspects of personal and social life. While the desire and the ability to learn are not shared equally by everyone, both can be fostered by good teaching, by careful guidance, by building and enlarging sympathetic enclaves, and by providing a range of educational efforts. These tasks are too great for partial and divided efforts (p. 82).

Evaluation and Critique

If endurance is any guide, then Houle's book must be judged to have had a lasting effect on the field of adult education. Over the years, since its original publication, the book has attracted a steady stream of citations in the literature, and in 1988 — long out of print in the original edition — it was reissued in facsimile with a Foreword by Long and an interesting and reflective Afterword by Houle himself.

Although there were other significant adult education books around at the same time as *The Inquiring Mind*, few have aged as well and as strongly as Houle's work (for example, Brunner, 1959; Burns, 1964; Jensen, Liveright & Hallenbeck, 1964; Kuhlen, 1963; Verner & Booth, 1964).

While *The Inquiring Mind* may not have become as popular or as well-known to general readers as, for instance, Overstreet's *The Mature Mind* (1949) or Riesman's *The Lonely Crowd* (1950), it did nevertheless form the basis of a series of 12 programs broadcast by public television, and it became what it is today, virtually required reading for any person undertaking serious study in adult education. In particular, as mentioned earlier, it gave new impetus and direction to two major streams of scholarly work: that concerned with participation in structured forms of adult education and that concerned with adult self-directed learning, or as Houle calls it, "self-education" or "auto-didactics" (p. 12). I will not dwell on the first of these two themes except to say that the typology of motivations has been subjected to exhaustive probing — often by sophisticated statistical procedures — and has been endorsed and elaborated by some, criticized or even rejected outright by others.

Of greater relevance to this present project however, is the fact that *The Inquiring Mind* stands at the head of an enormous research tradition, of which Allen Tough is probably the other best known, contemporary exponent. Tough (whose own work is reviewed in Chapters 6, 7, and 8 of this book) traces the origins of his interest in self-directed learning to a time in January, 1963, "when he received an assignment in a graduate course taught by Professor Cyril O. Houle at the University of Chicago" (1967, p. 1). Houle provides a matching perception in the Afterword to the second edition:

> The most prominent investigator in this field has been Allen Tough, the Canadian scholar, whose work has been augmented by his students and later their students. When first gaining a grasp of this theme, Tough read The Inquiring Mind as well as some of the transcripts of the 22 long interviews analyzed in it. He thereby found illustrations of the phenomenon he was later to study. More than that, he gained reinforcement of his conviction that an investigator could precisely analyze the self-directed learning actions of an individual (p. 92).

I have argued elsewhere (Candy, 1991) that this attempt to "precisely analyze the self-directed learning actions of an individual" may

well have been premature, if not entirely inappropriate. But that can
hardly be blamed on Houle's book as much as on the dominant desire
to quantify and measure phenomena — even when they are not
amenable to such reductionism.

Although the book has had an undoubted role in redefining the
major concerns of many adult educators, it has not been without its
critics. For instance, in a fairly savage early review of the book,
Warner was critical of the fact that Houle "interviewed and submitted
questionnaires to only some twenty-two Chicagoans" (p. 148). He
claims that the three-part typology is not just the central but indeed
"the only message" in the book and questions "the necessity of an
entire book's being fabricated on such skimpy material" (p. 148).
Furthermore, he takes issue with the view that all learning is equally
valuable: "To claim that the study of typing or driver education is as
important as that of history or philosophy is both foolhardy and igno-
rant" (p. 149), and accordingly he chides Houle for his "insistent plea
for social sanction to all those who wish to learn" (p. 149). This,
Warner claims, "smacks of our nation-wide neurosis for popularity.
We love to be loved and hate to be scorned, be it for foreign aid or
Fandancing II" (p. 149).

A much more muted criticism is offered by Benne who reviewed
the book for the *Journal of Higher Education*. Benne notes that "A
critic might quibble with Mr. Houle's system of categories. The distinction between 'goal-oriented' and 'learning-oriented' learners may,
for example, be more of an epistemological than a motivational distinction. And his class of 'activity'-oriented learners seems something
of a residual category bundling together a bewildering variety of
motivations for participation" (pp. 116-17). Despite this observation,
however, Benne's review is basically favorable and concludes with an
optimistic prognosis for the book's value to educators.

Williams (1963), in a predominantly positive and supportive
review after briefly summarizing and commenting on the content of
the book, turns his attention to its tone and style:

> The style throughout is clear and lucid, the arguments per-
> suasively put, and refreshingly devoid of that jargon that so
> frequently characterizes writing in this field. Professor
> Houle is, on occasion, carried away by his own eloquence,
> and particularly in the first of his three lectures lays him-
> self open to the accusation of disguising the thinness of the
> context with stylish elegance. This [however] is a minor
> blemish in a stimulating book . . . (p. 123).

More recently, Houle has been criticized by feminist scholars for the allegedly sexist tone of his writing and by critical theorists for adopting a largely descriptive and apparently value-neutral point of view. While there may be some truth to both these allegations, the book must be viewed in its historical context, recognizing both the accepted norms of writing at the time, as well as its status as a very tentative exploration of issues which, prior to then, had not been generally considered worthy of scholarly study at all.

Conclusion

Back in 1963, one of the reviewers of Houle's book predicted that it would have an impact "in healthy and substantial disproportion to its modest dimensions" (Williams, 1963, p. 123), and this has indeed proven to be the case. Whatever its shortcomings, *The Inquiring Mind* has managed to capture the imagination of scholars and practitioners alike and consequently to establish itself as something of a classic in the field. *The Concise Oxford Dictionary* states that, to describe something as classic, three things are implied:

1. That it be first class and of acknowledged excellence.
2. That it be simple, harmonious [and], well-proportioned.
3. That it be of enduring value, unaffected by changing fashion.

It seems to me that *The Inquiring Mind* exhibits each of these qualities. Right from its original publication it was recognized as innovative and of high quality; it was applauded for its conciseness and elegance; and it has certainly proved to be of enduring value. Indeed, if anything, both the qualitative methodology employed and the sort of knowledge claims advanced by Houle are more acceptable now than they were when the book first appeared (Candy, 1991).

In his Afterword, written for the recently published second edition (1988), Houle takes the opportunity to contextualize the study both historically and personally, to reflect on what he saw as the major influences the book had effected, and to speculate on lines of practical action and inquiry that he felt it might have been encouraged but had not. It is unusual that an author has the opportunity to comment on the perceived significance of his own work and so I quote his observations at some length. With respect to the practical side, he notes that in his opinion,

> . . . counselors have not built the idea of orientation into their systems of offering help. Teachers have not rethought their instructional patterns to reach students

who differ fundamentally from one another in how they think about the values of education. The people who study and write about adult education have not taken into account their own personal orientations (p. 94).

With respect to additional research that might have been stimulated by the book, Houle offers the following possible questions: "What is the process by which an adult who has not previously been engaged in purposeful learning begins to do so?" "How significant are 'learning enclaves' in the continuing pursuit of knowledge?" "How important are peer-stimulators in initiating the learning patterns of other people?" "Why . . . do avid learners usually fail to identify any of their school teachers or professors as significant influences in their development of the desire to learn, except when a personal or out-of-classroom relationship grew up?" "Why [are] some people, from their earliest days . . . driven to learn and others are not? . . . Here is a topic which calls for collaboration between the analysts of adult education and the experts of early childhood education and makes vividly meaningful the concept of lifelong learning." "And finally, how is an adult education program influenced by the orientation of its leader or leaders?" (pp. 97-98).

Thus, in reflecting back on the contribution of this remarkable book, we return to where we began: with questions. Although the scholarly study of self-directed learning has made enormous progress since the early 1960s, in many ways a number of fundamental and perennial questions remain unanswered. Each new wave of research has pushed out the limits of what we know about and how we can help adult self-directed learners but, paradoxically, like an archealogical dig, each layer removed reveals more to be explored and explained. All that is required is an inquiring mind.

References

Benne, K. D. (1962). Review of the inquiring mind. *Journal of Higher Education, 33*, 115-17.

Brilhart, J. K. (1963). Review of the inquiring mind. *Journal of general education, 14*, 275-75

Brunner, E. de S., et al. (1959). *An overview of adult education research.* Chicago, IL: Adult Education Association.

Burns, R. W. (Ed.). (1964). *Sociological backgrounds of adult education.* Chicago, IL: Center for the Study of Liberal Education for Adults.

Candy, P. C. (1991). *Self-direction for lifelong learning: A comprehensive guide to theory and practice.* San Francisco, CA: Jossey-Bass.

Craik, G. L. (1830-1). *The pursuit of knowledge under difficulties: Illustrated by anecdotes* (2 vols.). London, England: Published anonymously under the auspices of the Society for the Diffusion of Useful Knowledge.

Hawes, M. E. (1962). Review of the inquiring mind. *Library Quarterly, 32,* 109-110.

Houle, C. O. (1961). *The inquiring mind: A study of the adult who continues to learn.* Madison: University of Wisconsin Press (reprinted in facsimile, with a Foreword by H. B. Long and an Afterword by C. O. Houle, 1988, Norman, Oklahoma Research Center for Continuing Professional and Higher Education).

Jensen, G. E., Liveright, A. A., & Hallenbeck, W. (Eds.). (1964). *Adult education: Outlines of an emerging field of university study.* Washington, DC: Adult Education Association of the United States of America.

Knight, C. (1864-5). *Passages of a working life during half a century, with a prelude of early reminiscences* (3 vols.). London, England: Bradbury and Evans.

Kuhlen, R. G. (Ed.). (1963). *Psychological backgrounds of adult education.* Chicago, IL: Center for the Study of Liberal Education for Adults.

Oboler, E. M. (1961). Review of the inquiring mind. *Library Journal, 86*(13), 2465.

Overstreet, H. A. (1949). *The mature mind.* New York, NY: Norton.

Riesman, D. (1950). *The lonely crowd.* New Haven, CT: Yale University Press.

Ruddock, R. (1961). Review of the inquiring mind. *Adult Education* (UK), *34,* 222-24.

Tough, A. M. (1967). *Learning without a teacher: A study of tasks and assistance during adult self-teaching projects.* Educational Research Series No. 3. Toronto, Ontario: Ontario Institute for Studies in Education.

Verner, C., & Booth, A. (1964). *Adult education.* New York, NY: Center for Applied Research in Education.

Warner, J. F., Jr. (1962). Review of the inquiring mind. *Harvard Educational Review, 32,* 147-49.

Williams, D. C. (1963). Review of the inquiring mind. *Adult Education* (US), *13,* 122-23.

Chapter Five

Self-Directed Learning: A Guide for Learners and Teachers

Huey B. Long on Malcolm S. Knowles

Dr. Long is a W. K. Kellogg Professor of Adult Education at The University of Oklahoma. Over the period of the last several years, he has provided much of the leadership required to mount the six annual international symposia on self-directed learning that have been held to date. A recent review of the literature in the field of self-directed learning revealed that he has published over 25 works on the subject.

Self-Directed Learning: A Guide for Learners and Teachers is one of those basic books that should be read by anyone interested in self-directed learning. Staff developers and trainers should find the book as useful as educators in schools and colleges. The major emphasis is upon the learner engaged in group learning, but the information provided on contract learning can be applied equally well to other learner relationships.

This chapter is designed to provide a useful descriptive essay of the book. The following discussion has eight main divisions: (1) introduction, (2) andragogical origins, (3) overview of the book, (4) part one, the learner, (5) part two, the teacher, (6) part three, learning resources, (7) appendix, and (8) summary. Descriptive information concerning the book should be informative to most readers desiring to know more about self-directed learning. This descriptive essay, however, cannot substitute for the book itself. Read it.

Introduction

Self-Directed Learning: A Guide for Learners and Teachers by Malcolm Knowles is vintage Knowles. It is a small book of approximately 5 x 7 inches containing 135 pages. Fifty-eight pages are devoted to content and the remainder is devoted to what Knowles describes as learning resources.

Following the orientation, Knowles divides the book into four parts. Part I, identified as "The Learner," addresses seven topics in approximately 20 pages. Part II, written for the teacher, addresses four major topics in 30 pages. Part III, learning resources, constitutes the largest section of the book. Fifteen learning resources are provided in this division. An Appendix concludes the book. Each section is discussed in the narrative that follows. Before discussing the contents however, it is desirable to place the work within a historical context.

Andragogical Origins

Knowles' interest in self-directed learning is closely related to the development of andragogical philosophy: the art and science of teaching adults. Knowles' first major presentation on andragogy was in a speech delivered at West Georgia College in 1967. His next major contribution, which expanded his ideas on andragogy, was *The Modern Practice of Adult Education: Andragogy versus Pedagogy* (1970). This was later revised with a slightly different subtitle, *The Modern Practice of Adult Education: From Pedagogy to Andragogy* (1980). *Self-directed Learning: A Guide for Learners and Teachers* elaborates one of the major propositions included in andragogical philosophy: the nature of the adult learner. Specifically, according to Knowles, the adult learner is an individual who moves from a state of dependence to increasing independence in learning. Given that hypothesis, it was easy for Knowles to move into a teaching-learning strategy that emphasized self-directed learning. His personal orientation concerning self-directed learning is revealed through his heavy use of small group activity in his own public presentations and by his emphasis on learning resource materials in his publications. Thus, it is no accident that 57% of the pages in *Self-directed Learning: A Guide for Learners and Teachers* are devoted to learning resource materials while 43% of the pages are devoted to didactic content.

Malcolm's early work in self-directed learning closely parallels the learning projects work that Allen Tough conducted during the same period. It is important, however, to note that Tough and Knowles were dealing with different dimensions of the teaching-learning transaction. Tough's emphasis was more upon the *individual,* and his learner-oriented approach emphasized the learner to the point of almost neglecting the teacher or relegating the learner-teacher relationship to an occasional contact. In contrast, Knowles' interest was in the learner who often engaged in some kind of *group* learning activity, such as classroom learning. As a result, Knowles has more to say about the teacher's relationship to the learner than does Tough. With this brief historical framework established, we can now move into a discussion of *Self-directed Learning: A Guide for Learners and Teachers.*

The Book

Early in the book Knowles communicates his position concerning the role of the teacher. He suggests that learners may read the book without using the word *teacher,* as he does in the narrative. Accordingly, he suggests that "helper of any kind" (p. 7) may be substituted for teacher. He also quickly reveals his penchant for placing responsibility for learning with the learner. He says "in any case, you will soon discover that this is not a book to be read and reacted to. It is a resource for you to use as a self-directed learner, whether you are a student or a teacher. Make it work for You!" (p. 7). Knowles follows his own advice in emphasizing the importance of climate setting. Consistently throughout his career he has made a practice of emphasizing climate setting. He follows this practice in Part I with an effort to establish what he describes as a warm climate. He devotes several paragraphs to communicating respect and concern for the learner, in this instance the reader of the book, and he establishes a supportive and encouraging relationship with the reader. Finally, he seeks to establish what he calls a climate of mutual trust. He reveals his bias that self-directed learning is the best way to learn. He acknowledges that there are situations when what he describes as teaching, instruction, and even indoctrination may be called for, but he strongly takes the position that every act of teaching should have built into it some provision for helping the learner become more self-directing.

Part One — The Learner

This chapter contains two topics: diagnosing needs for learning and designing a lesson plan. The section on diagnosing the needs for learning focuses on the possibility that the learner has a need for a better understanding of self-directed learning. Accordingly, appropriate learning resources and other materials in the remaining sections of the book are discussed. He follows with the section on how to design a learning plan, which involves Inquiry Project Number Four, discussed later. Once again, at the conclusion of this brief chapter, we find Knowles' personality and his enthusiasm for self-directed learning revealed. He ends the chapter with the exhortation "happy adventuring" (p. 13).

Four inquiry projects devoted to the learner are included in this section of the book. The projects are titled as follows: Why Self-Directed Learning?; What is Self-Directed Learning?; What Competencies are Required for Self-Directed Learning?; and Designing a Learning Plan. These projects, as described, vary in length from approximately four brief paragraphs to several pages. Major ideas included in each learning project or each inquiry project are discussed below.

Inquiry Project Number One: Why Self-Directed Learning?

Three reasons for self-directed learning, along with three implications, are identified in this inquiry project. The reasons are as follows:

1. "Individuals who take the initiative in learning, learn more things, and learn better, than do people who sit at the feet of teachers possibly waiting to be taught . . ."(p. 14).
2. "Self-directed learning is more in tune with our natural processes of psychological development" (p. 14).
3. "Many of the new developments in education . . . put a heavy responsibility on the learners to take a good deal of initiative in their own learning" (p. 15).

The three implications identified are:

1. "It is no longer realistic to define the purpose of education as transmitting what is known" (p. 15).
2. "There must be somewhat different ways of thinking about learning" (p. 16).
3. "It is no longer appropriate to equate education with youth" (p. 16).

He summarizes the "why" of self-directed learning as survival. He indicates that individual survival and human survival are dependent upon self-directed learning. Knowles' comments in this area could be summed up as recommending self-directed learning because it is, in his opinion, basically more effective.

Inquiry Project Number Two: What is Self-Directed Learning?

In the discussion of this inquiry project, Knowles follows a position that he adopted in the first edition of *The Modern Practice of Adult Education* wherein he contrasts andragogy and pedagogy. Unfortunately, the contrasting approach used in this section of the book distracts the reader from Knowles' major assumptions that underlie self-directed learning. He identifies five major assumptions that are obscured in the effort to contrast self-directed learning with teacher-directed learning. Therefore, we should not be concerned here with the characteristics of teacher-directed learning. Instead, the emphasis is upon the five positive assumptions underlying self-directed learning. They are as follows:

1. "Self-directed learning assumes that the human being grows in capacity and needs to be self-directing as an essential component in maturing, and that this capacity should be nurtured to develop as rapidly as possible" (p. 20).
2. "Self-directed learning assumes that the learners' experiences become an increasingly rich resource for learning that should be exploited along with the resources of experts" (p. 20).
3. "Self-directed learning assumes that individuals become ready to learn what is required to perform their evolving life task or to cope more adequately with their life problems, and that each individual therefore has a somewhat different pattern of readiness from other individuals" (p. 20).
4. "Self-directed learning assumes that this orientation (learning as accumulating subject matter) is a result of their previous conditioning in school and that their natural orientation is task- or problem-centered, and that therefore learning experience should be organized as task-accomplishing or problem-solving learning projects (or inquiry units)" (p. 20-21).
5. "Self-directed learning assumes that learners are motivated by internal incentives such as the need for esteem (especially self-esteem), the desire to achieve, the urge to grow, the satisfaction of accomplishment, the need to know something specific, and curiosity" (p. 21).

The point is made that there may be situations where teacher-directed learning is to be preferred over self-directed learning. But even here Knowles continues to emphasize learner responsibility and critical thought. He indicates that there may be learning situations in which the learners' experience is of little worth: (1) when they have had no previous experience within that area of inquiry; (2) in areas where readiness to learn may be determined by one's level of matura-tion regarding the topic; (3) when the learner is required to focus on accumulating subject matter; and (4) in situations in which the learner is motivated by external pressures. Even under these circum-stances, Knowles observes "if self-directed learners recognize that there are occasions on which they will need to be taught, they will enter into those taught-learning situations in a searching, probing frame of mind and will exploit them as resources for learning without losing their self-directedness" (p. 21).

Inquiry Project Number Three: What Competencies are Required for Self-Directed Learning?

With this inquiry project, Knowles shifts from the didactic pre-sentation to a more learner-centered activity. The didactic material is limited to four brief paragraphs with the learner, or reader in this instance, given responsibility for analyzing his or her own learning competencies.

Resources

The resource section of the book contains nine competences that Knowles identifies with self-directed learning. Resource B is a self-rating instrument that provides the reader with the opportunity to assess the degree to which each competency is possessed. I have clas-sified the nine competences provided by Knowles into three types. They are cognitive, inter-personal, and personal. Five of the compe-tences are cognitive, two are interpersonal, and one is of a personal nature. Competency seven, "the ability to identify human and mate-rial resources appropriate to different kinds of learning objectives" (p. 41), is described, according to my system, as both an interpersonal and a cognitive competence because it requires the ability to identify human resources as well as non-human resources.

Knowles' list of competences contains a serious omission in my opinion. The list fails to include what I have noted in previous research as processing skills (Long, 1990). Processing skills include the ability to read, write, draw, sketch, observe, and other means by which an individual observes, records, and interprets information. It appears that these competencies are basic to most of the competencies in Knowles' list. Perhaps he made the assumption that all self-directed learners would automatically possess these abilities. I am of the opinion, however, that the processing skills need to be identified as sharply and as prominently as the other competencies.

Inquiry Project Number Four: Designing a Learning Plan

With this inquiry project, Knowles completes the transition from the instructional emphasis that characterizes Project One to a focus on learner activity in this project. Project Four primarily provides a guide to the development of a learning contract. Accordingly, the reader-learner is referred to Learning Resource C. The learner is expected to follow the instructions, which are provided in six or seven steps, to develop a personal learning contract.

Part Two — The Teacher

The 29 page section Knowles developed specifically for the teacher is described as an adventure in turning students onto learning. Once again, Knowles devotes some effort to set a climate for the teacher-writer or reader-writer relationship. Following the climate-setting activity he addresses sub-topics: (1) defining a new role, (2) developing self-directed learners, and (3) implementing the role of facilitator. The section structure, similar to that followed in the learners' section, is revealed in Part Two as the material progresses from more didactic narrative to greater involvement of the reader in suggested activities.

Defining a New Role

In this brief chapter Knowles discusses the dissonance he encountered in his own role when he began experimenting with encouraging students to be self-directed learners. He indicates that he had to change his ideas, which were originally based on four questions associated with teaching, to seven tasks he identifies with facilitating self-directed learning. The four questions that influenced his original ideas about teaching are as follows:

1. "What content needs to be covered?"
2. "How can this content be organized into manageable units?"
3. "How can these units be organized into a logical sequence?"
4. "What means of transmission will be most effective for transmitting each unit?" (pp. 31-32).

He then identifies seven tasks that he believes are required to implement the change from the teacher concept to that of facilitator of learning. They are as follows:

1. Climate setting.
2. Planning.
3. Diagnosing needs for learning.
4. Setting goals.
5. Designing a learning plan.
6. Engaging in learning activities.
7. Evaluating learning outcomes.

In addition to the seven specific tasks, he also identifies some psychological changes that he had to address. First, it required that he focus on what was happening in the student rather than on what he was doing. It also required that he divest himself of the protective shield of an authority figure and expose himself as an authentic human being with feelings, hopes, aspirations, insecurities, worries, strengths, and weaknesses. Furthermore, it required him to be clear about what resources he possessed that might be useful to the learners. As a result, he found himself performing quite a different set of functions, from those involved in transmitting information to those facilitating the inquiry design.

Knowles is candid in recognizing that teacher role change is accomplished with some difficulty. He identifies three problems and lists his solutions to them. Briefly stated the problems are: (1) structure versus non-structure, (2) content versus no content, and (3) how goals will be arrived at fairly? In response to the first problem, his position is that self-directed learning is not structureless but is an activity that requires a structure different from that used in traditional, pedagogical settings. His solution to the issue of content versus no content or content versus process is addressed by his position that self-directed learning addresses the *acquisition* of content rather than the *transmission* of content. Finally, he identifies the learning contract discussed in section one concerning the learner, Inquiry Project Number Four, as the solution to evaluation problems.

Developing Self-Directed Learners

This chapter is provided as a brief guide that the facilitator can use in developing self-directed learning in a classroom activity. Four optional strategies that might be used for this purpose are identified. It should be no surprise that *Self-Directed Learning: A Guide for Learners and Teachers* is recommended as a resource book for each of the strategies. Basically, the strategies all involve learners in some kind of interaction with content that is available in the book. The main difference in the strategies concerns the way the students are organized to engage in the activity. For example, one option is for the students individually to complete Inquiry Projects One through Four. Option number three describes a situation where all members of a given group of students would be involved in an intensive, two-day workshop on self-directed learning. The fourth option is a plan that is based on an orientation session conducted by the instructor prior to the actual beginning of the instruction. Options directly follow the outline of the book, whereas option four follows a different outline. Nevertheless, all options appear to require the use of learning resources included in the book or similar materials.

Implementing the Role of Facilitator

The final chapter in Part Two, written for the teacher, is a personal description provided by Knowles. In this chapter he describes his performance in a graduate course titled "The Nature of Adult Education." He indirectly cautions the reader that the procedures and activities may vary according to different factors.

The introductory section titled "Implementing the Role of Facilitator and Other Variables" describes the course as one that meets three hours each week for 15 weeks. The first five meetings, as described by Knowles, are generally planning meetings, with the first meeting devoted to an orientation, climate setting, and relationship-building activities. The second session is devoted to a diagnosis of needs for learning and formulating objectives. The third meeting, devoted to designing of learning plans, includes the preparation of learning contracts and the development of inquiry teams where students work together. The fourth session is devoted to contract revision and team planning. The fifth, sixth, and seventh meetings are devoted to team work activity as the team members discuss and pursue their inquiry topics and set a schedule for the presentation of their learning experiences, which will be made in sessions 8-13. At meeting 14, students are formed into groups of three, wherein each group member provides evidence of successful completion of the learning contract. Each team member provides consultive advice to the other two. The final meeting is devoted to course evaluation.

Part Three — Learning Resources

As noted earlier, the majority of *Self-directed Learning: A Guide for Learners and Teachers* consists of learning resources. The resources are presented in six different categories. At least two learning resources appear in each category except the one concerned with objectives. The categories are labeled as follows: general, climate setting in relationship building, diagnosing learning needs, formulating objectives, using learning strategies and resources, and evaluation.

Appendix

In addition to the learning resources mentioned above, the Appendix contains guidelines for contract learning. Two topics are discussed in the Appendix. The first addresses the question of why contract learning. The second tells how to develop a learning contract. The value of the learning contract is to be found in its reconciliation of imposed requirements from institutions with learners' needs to be self-directing, according to Knowles. In his view it blends the social requirements of most educational programs with learners' personal goals and objectives. The contract provides learners with a choice of means by which learning goals can be achieved and also provides options for measuring their progress toward achieving their goals.

In his discussion of the process used to develop a learning contract, five steps are identified. They are as follows:

Step 1   Includes a familiarization with course objectives, references concerning the objectives, and a list of inquiry units specifying the kinds of questions with which the course deals.

Step 2   Requires the learner to complete a set of blank contract forms along with some examples of contracts from previous courses. Learners have the option of completing a contract for an A grade or a B grade.

Step 3   Involves the selection of a consultation team of peers. Each member of the team will have a chance to review his or her contract with other members of the team to obtain reactions and suggestions.

Step 4   Includes the pursuit of the learning goals through selected
          strategies and the collection of evidence to be validated as
          specified in the learning contract.
Step 5   Is the review of the evidence submitted to support the
          learning contract activities.

Summary

Knowles' little book, *Self-Directed Learning: A Guide for Learners
and Teachers,* is a classic contribution to the literature of self-directed
learning. It is a book with which every individual who is interested in
self-directed learning should be acquainted. It is vintage Knowles in
that it captures the philosophy and practice of Malcolm Knowles.
Either by design or by accident, the arrangement of material flows
from an instructional didactic beginning to a more learner-oriented
activity.

The division of the book into three major sections also serves to
reflect the relationships involved in self-directed learning, the learner,
the teacher, and resource material. Some could argue about whether
the material accurately reflects the appropriate relationships in terms
of the content. Nevertheless, the book is an important, basic resource
in self-directed learning.

Implications for Trainers

Self-directed Learning: A Guide for Learners and Teachers contains
several implications for trainers. Five of the more important ones are
presented below.

1. The book underscores the importance of designing every learn-
    ing activity in such a way that it encourages and supports learn-
    ers' self-motivating and self-directing propensities.
2. Knowles makes us aware of the possibility that some learners
    have lost some of their desire and awareness of their self-direct-
    ing learning ability.
3. Learners whose readiness to assume self-directing learning
    behavior has been constrained by past practice, will need some
    encouragement in what for them may be a new way of learning.
4. Trainers whose experience has been dominated by behaviorally
    influenced teaching plans and whose attitudes reflect strict
    trainer control, may need some assistance in adopting methods
    that support self-directed learning.

5. Learners and trainers may be uncomfortable with the self-directed learning approach until they gain experience with it.

References

Knowles, M. S. (1967). *Andragogy not pedagogy.* Delbert Clark Award Address, West Georgia College, Carrolton, GA.

Knowles, M. S. (1968). Andragogy to pedagogy. *Adult Leadership, 16*(10), 352-352, 386.

Knowles, M. S. (1970). *The modern practice of adult education: Andragogy versus pedagogy.* New York, NY: Association Press.

Knowles, M. S. (1975). *Self-directed learning: A guide for learners and teachers.* Chicago, IL: Follett Publishing Co.

Knowles, M. S. (1980). *The modern practice of adult education: From pedagogy to andragogy.* New York, NY: Cambridge Books

Long, H. B. (1990). Peter the Great: A social-historical analysis of self-education principles. *Adult Education Research Conference Proceedings.* University of Georgia, Athens, GA.

Chapter Six

Major Learning Efforts: Recent Research and Future Directions

L. Adrianne Bonham on Allen Tough

Dr. Bonham is Assistant Professor of Adult and Extension Education at Texas A&M University. She has published several works in the field of self-directed learning and has served as Chairperson of the Task Force on Self-Directed Learning of the Commission of Professors of Adult Education.

Allen Tough teaches adult education at the Ontario Institute for Studies in Education, Toronto, Ontario, Canada; from that vantage point he has done research on adult self-directed learning for about as long as such learning has been a research concern in adult education. His peers' perceptions of the value of his work is clear: Three of the twelve pieces summarized in this book are by Tough.

The article discussed here, the earliest of Tough's contributions to this volume, did not so much make a new contribution to theory development as signify a major line of research that was already affecting theory development. More than a decade earlier Tough had begun a line of research with his dissertation. From that dissertation came an interview protocol that became a mainstay in research on adult learning activities. Using this approach, the trained interviewer took at least an hour to ask questions and probe about learning that the person had done during the previous year.

The Article Summarized

Tough's article, which appeared in *Adult Education*, summarized existing research under headings of basic surveys; geographical areas; occupational categories; educational level; peer groups; and motivation, tasks, and help.

Basic surveys showed there is a great deal of consistency among

adult populations in terms of the learning projects that people conduct. A learning project was defined by Tough as "a highly deliberate
effort to gain and retain certain definite knowledge and skill, or to
change in some other way" (Tough, 1978, p. 250). Operationally it
was defined as an effort of at least seven hours duration; in fact, the
research found that the average project took 100 hours. On average a
learner was found to conduct five such projects per year — spending
almost 10 hours per week on learning projects. Not only was the
average high, but it was estimated that 90% of all adults conduct at
least one learning project per year.

The careful reader will note that, to this point, no distinction has
been made between self-directed learning and other-directed learning. The first contribution made by Tough's line of research was to
establish that a great many adults do a great many things — and
commit many hours — in order to learn. The second contribution
was to determine that for much of that learning — 80% of it — an
amateur does the day-to-day planning. Furthermore in 73% of the
learning, the amateur who does the planning is the learner.

The complete breakdown was: 73% self-planned; 20% planned by
professionals (including group or class, 10%); one-on-one helper, 7%;
nonhuman source, such as programmed instruction, 3%; 4% planned
by peers in a group; and 3% planned for the individual by a friend
(see figure 6.1). Tough also noted that, while some projects were
excluded from calculations because they involved more than one category, all excluded projects included some self-planning.

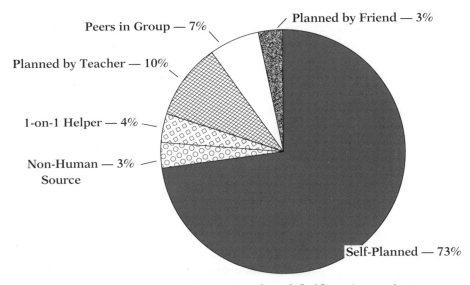

Figure 6.1 Sources of planning for adults' learning projects.

Tough also reported that, for all types of learning projects, the chief motivation was goal oriented; fewer projects were done for the love of learning. Tough did not mention learning for the sake of activity. Thus he completely or largely discounted two of the three categories of learners mentioned by Houle (Chapter 4). Under another heading in the article, Tough reported two studies that listed personal development and self-fulfillment as top reasons for learning; he did not acknowledge or discuss the fact that these studies seemed not to support his generalization that the chief motivation was goal oriented.

The geographic areas covered by research in Tough's review included Jamaica, Ghana, New Zealand, Tennessee, Nebraska, and the United States as a whole. The research dealt with all types of learning projects, not just those that were self-directed.

The U. S. study found that people had a variety of reasons for choosing to learn on their own. Top reasons were the desires of learners to learn at their own pace, in their own style, in flexible ways, and according to their own structure. Traditionally cited barriers to participation in adult education — lack of a class, lack of time or money, etc. — were on the list but not at the top. This study also found that while magnitude of difference was quite small, the persons most likely to have made at least one self-planned learning effort were female, young, White, well-educated, of higher income level, and of higher self-reported social class.

In terms of occupational categories, Tough described studies that involved unemployed adults, mothers of preschool children, professional men, schoolteachers (in the United States, Canada, and Ghana), Cooperative Extension agents, college and university administrators, parish ministers, and pharmacists. While he did not draw conclusions, the summary hints that such occupational groupings may be important in defining at least the content of adult learning and perhaps the ways adults choose to learn.

Studies cited in relation to educational level led to the conclusion that learning is a characteristic of adults with low educational level, as well as of those with more formal education. Peer groups were found to facilitate a wide range of learning for adults.

The topics included in Tough's section on motivation, tasks, and help identified several key issues that would be explored further by Tough and others in the following decade. Several studies sought reasons for beginning or continuing learning projects or explored the amount and kind of help secured from other people when learning projects were self-planned.

The subject that had the greatest impact on future research, however, was the actual process used by learners in planning their own

learning. "In self-planned learning," said Tough, "the adult must perform many of the planning tasks that would be performed by the
instructor during a course" (p. 258). He mentioned several studies
that produced detailed lists of the planning tasks undertaken by
learners. Later in this discussion, in evaluating the impact of this
chapter and the research line it represents, we will return to Tough's
statement about planning.

A final section in Tough's article identified directions for further
action and study. Adult educators were encouraged to produce
printed materials and offer group and individual instruction to help
learners gain skill in planning their learning. Public policies studies
and action were suggested to facilitate the kinds of learning projects
done by adults. Tough suggested more study like what had been
done — global studies of adults' learning projects and of other kinds
of intentional change, studies of what motivates people to undertake
long-term learning projects, and studies of how to facilitate learning
by peer self-help groups.

Implications for Theory and Practice

Allen Tough contributed a significant set of findings to the process of theory development about adult self-directed learning.
Decades earlier E. L. Thorndike had shown empirically that adults
could learn — a new thought for his day (Thorndike, Bregman,
Tilton, & Woodyard, 1928). Allen Tough showed empirically that
adults *do* learn in deliberate and extensive ways — a new thought for
his day. Furthermore, Tough showed the large degree to which such
learning is planned by the learner and not by an educational institution or trained professional. He pointed out that one role for an adult
educator is to help adults gain the skills needed in order to learn with
maximum effectiveness when they learn on their own.

Tough suggested a considerable change of focus — or at least the
addition of a second focus — for those of us who are professionals
expected to teach and train adults. He implied that we should not
limit ourselves to being purveyors of content but should coach adults
to teach themselves.

What would this change of focus mean to the corporate trainer,
for instance, who usually designs conferences and workshops to
update workers on job skills? It might mean planning some workshops on learning how to learn. Or devoting a large portion of time
to individual conferences to coach workers in learning skills and
strategies. Or devoting more of the budget to software (including
print on paper) that learners can use by themselves. Or helping to

establish a corporate environment where it is acceptable for one employee to use another employee as a learning source — on company time.

What does Tough's article imply about the range of content that should be the concern of corporate trainers? It has already been mentioned that Tough may have overstated the case for learning being goal-oriented. Even if that is not so, his list of goals that motivate learning includes many that relate to adult roles other than that of worker. People want to know how to raise a child, teach a church school class, repair something around the house, sew a dress, perform a sport or leisure activity, or conduct a successful political campaign. While these concerns will never be the chief concern of the corporate trainer, there are reasons the trainer should deal with them to some extent. They contribute to the overall welfare of the worker; and they can be the content that the worker uses to develop learning skills that can be applied to work-related learning.

A Caution About Implications

Sometimes researchers who make valuable contributions also put themselves and others onto false scents, which they follow in vain. Some later researchers (for instance, Spear & Mocker, Chapter 9) have suggested that the false scent Tough followed had to do with how adults plan learning projects for themselves. While concern with process is not the major focus of this article by Tough (See Chapter 7, in which it is the major focus), his references to process anticipate the research reported elsewhere by Tough.

Contrasting the "amateur" planner with the "professional" planner (Tough's words and Tough's quotation marks) in terms of doing "the detailed day-to-day planning" (p. 252), he went on to the already quoted comparison of the amateur's planning to that done "by the instructor of a course" (p. 258). Tough then referred to an earlier publication of his in which he gave "a more detailed list of planning tasks" (p. 258). He cited another study that dealt in great detail with the learner's planning steps.

The relevant question here is, "Why should we assume that the amateur uses the same kind of process that the professional teacher uses?" Corollary questions include: Why should we assume that the untrained learner does naturally what the professional had to be taught to do; that the about-to-be-learner has to know the precise learning goal before starting to learn; that methods and resources are chosen after an analysis of the effectiveness of all available ones; that planning and conducting a learning project constitute a linear process that progresses from a known beginning to a known end?

It appears that Tough may have been a captive of his own history; after all, he teaches people to plan instruction for adults. He may also have been a captive of his methodology. An unstructured interview protocol leaves a great deal of freedom for the interviewer to probe for whatever answers he expects to get. In fact, Tough complained that some findings that did not fit his generalizations might be blamed on interviewers not having proper training in eliciting the expected results. Furthermore, most of us, if interviewed about actions as much as a year old, would probably remember them as being much more linear and purposeful than they were; so might research subjects being interviewed by well-trained interviewers. The results of such unstructured interviews also are susceptible to being interpreted according to preconceived ideas when it comes time to analyze the data.

Of course, it was not Tough's intention to follow a false scent. He obviously recognized the importance of understanding how amateurs do successful self-directed learning. He quoted himself as saying, "We must first understand how the learning proceeds in its natural form. Only then will we be ready to fit our help into that natural process without disrupting it" (p. 289).

While this discussion may seem important to researchers and theory builders, what is its meaning for practitioners? If we intend to help adults learn to be more self-directed in their learning — or more successful in their self-directed learning — we should not assume they need the skills that trainers use in planning conferences and workshops. We should look elsewhere for models of what happens naturally. Furthermore, if we are to help people gain natural kinds of skills, we may have to *use* some teaching-learning approaches that mimic what happens naturally. We may have to live with a certain amount of frustration in laying aside the linear planning we have learned to appreciate for its efficiency and clear objectives.

Summary

Allen Tough summarized research showing that adults dedicate a great deal of time to sustained learning projects and that most of those projects are planned by the learners themselves.

Implications for corporate trainers include the need to offer support to individuals to facilitate their self-planned learning. Such support may include individual and group guidance in developing needed skills, encouragement to value the learners' own efforts, provision of materials that learners can use alone, and creation of an atmosphere in which employees are encouraged to learn from one another.

References

Tough, A. (1978). Major learning efforts: Recent research and future directions. *Adult education, 28,* 250-263.

Thorndike, E. L., Bregman, E. O., Tilton, J. W., & Woodyard, E. (1928). *Adult learning.* NY: The Macmillan Company.

Chapter Seven

The Adult's Learning Projects: A Fresh Approach to Theory and Practice in Adult Learning, 2nd Edition

Carol E. Kasworm on Allen Tough

Dr. Kasworm is Associate Professor in the Department of Technological and Adult Education at The University of Tennessee, Knoxville. She has also served in administrative positions including Associate Vice Chancellor for Academic Affairs and Associate Provost for Faculty and Professional Development at The University of Houston, Clearlake. Her research interests have focused on self-directed learning across the lifespan and on adult undergraduate students as self-directed learners.

One of the key contributors to the theory and the practice of adult self-directed learning has been *The Adult's Learning Projects: A Fresh Approach to Theory and Practice in Adult Learning, 2nd Edition.* Written by Allen Tough, this book introduces the reader to the key concepts of adult learning projects and of self-planned (self-directed) learning. In addition, it provides a systematic, research-supported description on key resources, strategies, processes, and people interactions that support self-planned learning efforts. Beyond its personal reader impact, it has been cited for many valuable contributions to the national and international education community.

In this chapter I will share with you the historical context of Tough's work, the major elements of this book, and the current value of his work for professionals in human resource development. I will not address the latter portion of the book, the postscript section. I have elected to do this because much of the information covered in the postscript was covered in Tough's *Major Learning Efforts: Recent Research and Future Directions* (1978), which is summarized by Bonham in Chapter Six of this book.

Historical Context

Tough's initial interest focused upon "deliberate adult learning — self-planned learning." His own personal context for this work was initiated through his roles as a learner and teacher at the University of Toronto; his involvement in experiential, nonformal learning; and his related activities in the adult education community. During his doctoral research at University of Chicago with Dr. Cyril Houle, he focused this interest upon the behavior of adults while planning their own learning projects and conducting "self-teaching." His findings about adult self-teaching were presented in his doctoral dissertation and subsequently in *Learning Without a Teacher: A Study of Tasks and Assistance During Adult Self-Teaching Projects* (1967). (The updated revision of this work is discussed by O'Donnell in Chapter 8). As you will note, this earlier work and the current volume, *The Adult's Learning Projects*, have genuinely reflected the power of the adult to design and conduct significant learning without the direction of an expert instructor, institutional structures, or a formalized certification process. These works have presented a clear vision of the adult as his or her own decision-maker of learning and the learning process.

Although Tough continued to research and support activities in the area of adult learning projects, his more recent energies have focused on a broader horizon of adult learning. His later work, reflected in *Intentional Changes: A Fresh Approach to Helping People Change* (1982), built upon this concept of purposeful adult learning and of the strategies for making intentional changes in our adult lives.

The Adult's Learning Projects presents the first major, descriptive research study that identified the key elements of self-planned (self-directed) learning and the nature of adult learning projects. Although earlier works identified the concept that adults could learn without a formal classroom, most educators and trainers had difficulty in visualizing and understanding "learning without a teacher." Many researchers and educators dismissed his early work, believing that learning could only occur with the guidance of an "expert" in a formalized interaction between a teacher and a learner. However, due to the strength of his research framework, significant supportive research, and the salience of his ideas, Tough's research has become the "touchstone" . . . the basis for characterizing and understanding self-directed learning. Tough's pioneering research has provided the language, the concepts, and most importantly the descriptive terms for key elements and processes of self-planned learning.

The practitioner community has found this current volume, *The Adult's Learning Projects* (1979), invaluable. It has stimulated trainers, teachers, and resource consultants to rethink the adult learning process. Over the years Tough has encouraged researchers, students, and professionals to conduct their own investigations in this area. In particular, the HRD community has begun to consider the potency of self-directed learning in relation to worker acceptance of innovation, worker productivity, and worker autonomy. For example, recent research has shown that self-directed learner characteristics were positively correlated with performance in the workplace. In essence, workers who were self-directed learners were high performers when the organizational climate supported learning (York, 1991). Thus, current research investigations suggest the potency of self-directed learning for workplace performance, as well as continued enhancement of worker knowledge and skills.

Key Contributions and Definitive Ideas

This text models an implicit set of beliefs and values focused on the adult learning experience. These beliefs include:

1. Significant, powerful learning outcomes occur in self-planned learning.
2. Adults devote considerable time and energies in their self-planned learning projects.
3. Adults do not learn in isolation; they often work with others to plan, to learn, and to receive feedback in designing their self-planned learning.
4. Adults use a variety of resources in their self-planned efforts — people, written materials, visual/oral materials, pre-designed learning experiences, and active (trial and error) experiences.
5. Adults create, conduct, and evaluate their learning projects in relation to their self-defined needs and goals.
6. Learning projects are based in a collaborative and facilitative climate. Adults, as self-directed learners, seek resource support through a relationship of trust, encouragement, and feedback.

Within this broad discussion of beliefs, there are two interesting points about this work. In this book Tough moves from the notion of self-teaching to the central notion of self-planning. This shift from "teaching" to "planning" incorporates a broader perspective of the adult learner's actions and the learner's use of other resources, including the conventional classroom, to learn specific information or skills for a learning project. He does not use the term "self-directed" in his work. From my vantage point, I suspect that Tough found the term "self-planned" to speak more clearly to his concept of the role of the adult in relation to the myriad of forms and uses of planners, learning resources, and efforts to deliberately learn by one's-self. The term "self-directed" was suggested in Tough's writings but was given popular identity through the writings of Malcolm Knowles and others who also discussed the research and practice of adult self-learning. It should also be noted that Tough made a clear effort to speak to the learning projects of children and youth. Although his work and much of the literature speaks to adult self-planned or self-directed learning, Tough also desired to document the definitive efforts by children and youth to plan their own deliberate learning projects. Self-planned, self-directed learning is not just an adult action; it does not occur solely because of maturity, experiences, or cognitive maturation. He saw self-planned learning as a learning process throughout the lifespan.

Characteristics of Self-Planned Learning

The cornerstone of Tough's work was his characterization of self-planned learning. One of the key elements of this characterization was the "learning project." This term referred to:

> . . . a series of related episodes, adding up to at least seven hours. In each episode, more than half of the person's total motivation is to gain and retain certain fairly clear knowledge and skill, or to produce some other lasting change . . . (p. 7).

This term expressed a framework of commitment to learning, the learner's goal orientation, and the complex series of self-defined and directed learning experiences. Analogous to our terms of curriculum or learning plan, "learning project" reflected a label that captured the dynamic structures and actions in a self-directed learning journey.

When we organize courses for training programs, there are learning plans, objectives, and often pre- and post-assessment. We design our courses with a knowledge of the content, the learners, and the preferred outcomes. Thus, the design of learning is normally based upon a hierarchical, sequential structure of knowledge, skills, and experiences in relation to desired pre-defined outcomes. Contrary to these expert beliefs about curriculum design, self-directed learning starts from a different base of assumptions. Learning projects are created by a question, a goal, an outcome, an intention, or a desire. Thus, learning projects start from a point of entry into an often unknown and sometimes foggy territory of new knowledge and skill for the learner. Learning projects reflect a private and often evolving understanding of the learning pursuit. This process of designing a learning project is dynamic, circuitous, and filled with many stops, starts, and detours.

Tough suggests that each learning project is usually conducted in a series of *episodes*. Each episode reflects a specific period of time of individual actions; however, each episode is only one part of the broader, self-planned learning project. Some learning projects may extend over a period of years, with numerous episodes. Other learning projects may reflect one month of activity and be based in a few episodes of learner activity. For purposes of his definitional research study, Tough chose a minimum of seven hours of involvement for a learner activity to qualify as a learning project. This time commitment is somewhat arbitrary but reflects an adequate and sufficient investment in a learning outcome.

Each learning episode also reflected a very deliberate, focused period of time where the individual is motivated and is acting on the desire to gain and retain specific knowledge or skill. Tough used this notion of learning episode and learning project to aid adult learners in their characterization of self-planned and self-directed learning. In particular, self-planned learning is not incidental or spontaneous learning. Rather, the learner is deliberate in creating, planning, and acting on a learning project. Learning projects assume that adult learners are proactive rather than passive. Learners are organizers and regulators of the focus, action, and evaluation of learning experiences. Some educators and trainers have presumed that self-planned learning refers to independent, solitary, or isolated learning experiences. These conditions may be possibilities in specific learning projects, but they are not always represented in self-planned learning. Learning projects are created, conducted, and evaluated by the learner's executive control over the experiences. The learner may use other individuals or resources to aid in the planning, the conducting of learning experiences, and the evaluating of the project. What is unique in relation to our conventional notions of education is this "learner-control," the executive control over the learning project.

How Active are Adults in Learning Projects?

Tough presented a rather intriguing set of descriptive findings from his interviews with 200 individuals.

1. Most adults were actively engaged in self-planned learning projects.

2. These adults reported an annual range of 0 to 20 learning pro-
    jects; eight learning projects each year was the mean for each
    adult in this survey.
3. On average, each person expended about 700 to 800 hours a
    year on learning projects.
4. For each learning project the interviewed adults expended
    approximately 100 hours, with a median of 81 hours per project.

Focus of the Learning Projects

Major categories of learning projects reported in these interviews
include:

1. Preparing for and staying current in an occupation.
2. Specific tasks and problems on the job.
3. Learning for home and personal responsibilities.
4. Improving some broad area of competence.
5. Learning for interest or leisure.
6. Curiosity or a question about certain subject matter.

Most of the learning projects incorporated both the pragmatic
interest and application of knowledge and skills, along with the more
affective, global, and intellectual understandings. A vast number of
individuals noted that many of their learning projects were related to
their job or occupation. Clearly, many of these projects were concerned with preparation to enter into a particular job/occupation, as
well as with developing additional competence for advancement in
their work roles or for adapting to new technology introduced to the
workplace.

In addition to these broader categories, Tough also suggested that
learning projects were initiated in response to internal and external
changes within the learner. Internal forces focused on the learner's
interior adjustment to a changing role within the life cycle, to self-
appraisal and perspective change, to evolving responsibilities for children, family, job and community, and sometimes to adaptation to a
loss in one's life. External forces came from the changing and often
conflicting world of knowledge, technology, and values as it impacted
the learners. On occasion, learning projects were designed to produce or direct new changes in society. For example, some projects
were oriented towards the future, towards planning or producing personal or social changes of long-range impact. Tough noted that when
adults chose to pursue a new area of knowledge or skill, this decision
usually reflected one or more learning projects.

Why Do Adults Pursue Self-Planned Learning?

Adults engage in learning projects with different expectations, goals, and outcomes. Tough suggested that most adults engage in learning projects with fairly significant expectations. In essence, they conduct a learning project in order to be more successful, more competent, or more knowledgeable. Tough also found that many individuals also derived significant pleasure, satisfaction, and enhanced self-esteem from their learning projects. In these interviews adult learners reported improved performance and other externally rewarding influences from the project completion. The broad categories of reasons for involvement in learning projects include:

1. *Intention of using the knowledge and skill.* Adults enter learning projects with a wide variety of uses and applications in mind. Some individuals identify an immediate need and conduct a learning project expecting a clear end result. Other individuals are assigned a job task and need to identify the knowledge and skill required to achieve the assigned goal, as well as conduct the actual learning project. For others, their activities may alternate between learning and application throughout the learning project.

2. *Imparting the knowledge and skill.* This category is often the essence of why we learn new knowledge and skill, which is both to enhance our own performance and to influence others through formal and informal interactions and job responsibilities.

3. *Future understanding or learning.* Although we often find ourselves faced with an immediate problem for resolution or an immediate need for new knowledge in application, we also may consider the need for new knowledge/skill in future learning, understandings, and applications. As adults we are often able to see the benefits of future knowledge and skill to enhance our actions, understandings, and behavior.

4. *Pleasure, self-esteem, and confidence from possession.* Most adults who have completed learning projects believe that they now have a new sense of pleasure, self-esteem, or confidence in their newly acquired knowledge, skill, or understanding. They not only experienced pleasure in the learning process but also reported specific, affective benefits from the outcomes of a learning project.

5. *Learning for credit (verified expertise).* Certain individuals reported that they conducted learning projects that incorporated some form of credit, certification, or an examination related to one's job or occupation.

6. *Immediate benefits.* There are many immediate benefits that
    add to the learner's motivation at the beginning of and/or in the
    continuation of a learning project. However, these anticipated
    benefits do not depend on retaining the knowledge and skill for
    a number of days. On the contrary, there are immediate bene-
    fits during the process of the learning project. These benefits
    include:
    a. Satisfying curiosity, puzzlement, or a question.
    b. Enjoyment from the content itself.
    c. Enjoyment from practicing the skill.
    d. The activity of learning.
    e. Learning successfully.
    f. Completing unfinished learning.
    g. Aspects unrelated to learning, e.g., association with certain
        people, a change of routine, or a new activity or challenge.

How Does a Learning Project Occur?

To provide a relevant understanding of the process of a learning
project, I would like to discuss a hypothetical activity of an HRD consultant working with an adult self-directed learner. You (as an HRD
specialist) are meeting with a male adult learner (a supervisor of a
work crew) who "desires to gain a greater understanding of, appreciation for, and ability to work with cultural diversity." (This statement
regarding the learner's goals reflects our own language, concepts, and
jargon.) The supervisor comes to you to facilitate his own problem
solving and to begin a learning project. In your first meeting with
him, he states that he wants to know why a Hispanic worker doesn't
associate with the other members of the crew and appears ill at ease
with him as an Anglo supervisor. He suspects that the problem is the
cultural differences highlighted by the recent inclusion of Hispanics
into his work unit. In addition, you discuss with him other related
issues, concerns, and questions both to clarify and possibly to expand
his goals for this learning project. From this initial identification of
possible concerns, he proceeds to consult several other sources,
including two informative books on multicultural work supervision,
to define his particular learning project. After some private contem-
plation and perhaps discussion with a fellow supervisor and friend,
he becomes more definitive. A week later he comes back to you for
further discussion. He states that, as a supervisor, he wants to figure
out how to create a sense of trust, understanding, and good communication between himself as the supervisor, the work crew, and the
Hispanic workers. (At this point he has identified the focus of his

learning project. He has utilized you, his fellow supervisor, and several workbooks, as well as his own planning expertise for his development of learning project goals.)

How does he plan his learning project? He creates a series of explorations based on tentative beliefs and needs about this project. His first episode includes contacting the Human Resources Cultural Diversity Office to identify a trainer who "knows about Hispanic workers" and about "communications between Hispanics and Anglos." A trainer is identified who not only will act as a resource planner and expert for the supervisor but who also will provide other resources (books, videotapes on multicultural communications, short courses, as well as identify other supervisors who are involved in this topic of inquiry). The supervisor utilizes the HRD trainer as a resource consultant. The trainer assists the supervisor to clarify specific learning activities that will meet his objectives. The trainer also helps the supervisor plan strategies for learning. The supervisor will utilize these recommended learning resources, as well as go back to the workbooks on multicultural work supervision. The supervisor notes that these workbooks also suggest key topics, activities, and ideas for his learning project. Thus, these workbooks act as a resource consultant for both content and learning strategies.

In the development of a learning project, the adult learner utilizes *planners* (individuals, in the form of the trainer and his fellow supervisor, and non-human resources, such as the workbooks and videotapes) to help structure and guide him in his episodes of learning. Each planner helps the learner determine more narrowly defined learning goals, as well as specific resources and strategies that will meet his particular learning goals. These planners also may assist the learner to define the desired outcomes of this learning project and the varied activities he will use to evaluate his own performance with this new knowledge.

From the above example you will note that there is a lack of preciseness of terms, in part because the learner and the planners/consultants are dealing with an imprecise and vaguely defined area. This process is based within the learner and within an evolving learning journey. In fact, recent research suggests that learners who explore new and unknown territory (novice explorations) develop rather global and vague, initial learning plans. These initial plans are redefined with new information and developing expertise as learners reflect on this new information and their desired end goal. On the other hand, learners who are involved in learning projects that build upon their known expertise are more often precise, focused, and specific about their plans, actions, and evaluations.

After the planning process, the learner will assemble an action plan made up of a series of episodes (learning events). In this hypothetical scenario, the worker conducts readings, establishes a discussion with two informal leaders of his work team, and begins a mentoring program with the Hispanic workers. Completion of this plan reflectes sufficient episodes to meet the learning goals. However, the learner (supervisor) is continuously involved in this learning activity and in the application of new ideas, skills, and attitudes. Thus, this learning plan may also be changed or new learning projects created as the learner discovers new information, reflects on his current interactions with his multicultural workforce, or identifies new and highly relevant learning resources.

The Planning Process of a Learning Project

From the above example, it is evident that most learning projects are not begun with a complete, systematically developed plan. However, through his research, Tough identified key elements of all self-planned learning projects. These elements include:

1. Decision to begin (often referred to as goal-setting).
2. Choosing a planner(s) (resources to help define and support the learning activities).
3. Factors that influence the choice of and interactions with planners (rationale for selection of a particular planner, as well as the form and structure of the learning experiences).
4. Activities in the planning process (learning objectives, learning resources and strategies, and activities that provide validating feedback of learning outcomes).

Decision to Begin

Every learner goes through a preparatory series of steps in his/her decision to proceed with a learning project and in determining the particular knowledge and skill to be learned in that project. Tough identifies 26 steps in this preparatory process of decision making. Beyond this extensive elaboration, he more specifically notes that most of the adults in his research commented on the difficulties they faced in making the decision. They truly desired competent, facilitative, helpful assistance in clarifying their learning goals. Thus, one of the more crucial areas of effective learning project activity is *goal setting*.

Developing competence in goal setting is one of the significant challenges facing HRD practitioners. It is not just a matter of instructing adults in a decision-making, goal-setting process. Tough suggests that effective goal setting also incorporates a creative, intuitive expertise of self-assessment and self-action.

Choosing the Planner

As suggested earlier, learning projects are controlled and directed by the learner, not by an expert (a trainer, a supervisor, or a program designer). Adults engage in planning a learning project with the collaboration of planners. These planners aid the learner in making a majority of the decisions about what to learn and how to learn it, how to sequence it, how to manage time with deadlines, and how to identify expected intermediate/final outcomes. One of the key findings of Tough's research was the identification of four types of planners. These include:

1. *Learner himself/herself.* Two-thirds of the learning projects were planned by the learner. The remaining third of the projects were planned by the other three types of planners.
2. *Use of an object.* This is a nonhuman resource, such as a programmed instruction book, a set of tapes, a series of television programs, or a workbook, which aid in the planning of the learning project.
3. *Use of a person who interacts with the learner* on a one-to-one basis. This person might be an HRD trainer, a tutor, a supervisor/coach/mentor, a consultant, or other expert. It might be a friend, neighbor, relative, or colleague. This one-to-one interaction might also be more structured, such as private lessons, or a helpful, consultative discussion or mentoring process.
4. *Involvement in a group,* often with a leader or an instructor who aid in planning what and how to learn in the learning project. This group could be a network of peers, a training class or discussion group, a group led by a trained instructor, or a self-help educative group.

In addition, Tough reported that some learning projects reflected a mixed planner model . . . referring to a combination of several of the above types. Self-planned and mixed-planner projects were typically much longer in duration than the other types. Perhaps because of the greater length of involvement in self-planned and mixed projects, individuals reported that they saw greater magnitude of change or greater gains of new knowledge and skill from self-planned and mixed-planner projects.

Almost half of the interviewees conducted at least one project that was planned by a group or its leader, with a similar number of interviewees who conducted at least one project planned in a one-to-one relationship. One of the provocative findings of this study noted that only one-fifth (19%) of the projects were planned by a paid person or a person who was doing this as part of a job or as a volunteer responsibility in some agency. In essence, adult learners utilized trainers, HRD professionals, and other professional experts for only one in every five learning projects. These findings suggest we can be most effective with adult self-directed learners by helping them enhance their own self-directed learning abilities and skills.

Factors Influencing Choice of Planners and Resources

Key factors influencing choice of planners included efficiency, ease, access, cost, and personal preferences. Efficiency was often the most important criterion for these adults. Many individuals noted, "What is the fastest, easiest, cheapest way for me to learn the knowledge and skill that I want?" Each learner expressed specific preferences and values that influenced their decision. Clearly, they valued ease of access, ease in using a preferred learning format, and each valued multiple resource options.

Although these factors influenced the choice of planners, Tough found that there were a significant number of other concerns in the planning process and in the selection of a planner. Some learners did have the expertise to plan a learning project. However, they discovered that a learning project is a highly complex and delicate set of tasks. Some learners found themselves lacking specific knowledge and skills in the planning process. Some also had difficulty in the identification of learning goals, resources for learning, or evaluation strategies and feedback resources of their learning experiences. Although convenience, ease, and access were significant determiners, most learners faced serious difficulties in their initial pre-planning and planning efforts.

In most cases learners lacked information or some aspect of competence to plan and conduct the entire learning experience. Most learners sought out and relied upon friends, colleagues, or acquaintances. This consultative advice and feedback aided them in determining the appropriateness and effectiveness of their efforts. However, learners often found the need for varied expertise because of the need for both goal-setting consultants as well as learning strategy consultants. Goal-setting consultants would help the learner to identify and clarify the learning goals for the projects; strategy consultants would help the learner select a planner or identify when to use a planner in the learning project planning process.

Tough discovered that his surveyed learners had consulted at least four or five individuals through direct contact and interaction in their learning project. Some learners used as many as 10 to 20 individuals. These contacted consultants provided information, encouragement, advice, and perhaps subject matter to the learner. A few learners also created their own support learning network. They brought together fellow learners who were interested in the same type of learning activities. For example, certain personal, computer-user groups reflected this informal network of fellow learners who desired to exchange new information, instruct each other on new innovations, and share ideas on a common topic of interest.

Beyond the use of human resources, most individuals used and valued written and visual/oral materials that provided information, direction, and insight. Tough found that printed material was particularly common in the learning projects. Books, magazines, newspapers, workbooks, bibliographies, duplicated materials, and other written/printed forms of information proved very helpful. Many individuals also valued visual, pictorial, or auditory forms of learning (books on tape, music, speeches, observations, and modeling of viewed behavior).

On occasion some individuals also created a learning log resource to record their involvements and experiences. This log provided an opportunity to analyze, reflect, and gain insights regarding the planning and execution of personal learning projects.

The Value of Self-Planned Learning for the Adult Learner

Learning projects are significant time and identity investment activities. Often adults may value the easier route of a pre-designed course. However, research has amply demonstrated that adults do actively engage in their own learning projects. Adults make purposeful choices to learn on their own, without the support, direction, and instruction of professional educators, trainers, or experts. There are many reasons for these individual learning pursuits. One of the key reasons is that the learning project is more focused and more styled to the individual's knowledge level, expertise, and use or application goals. It is under the control of the learner and therefore can be paced for the intensity, duration, and particular physiological or psychological needs of the learner. Some learners cannot easily access expert-designed courses, programs, or materials. Thus access, cost, and other related factors of convenience to the learner support the route of self-directed learning. Some learners desire to use particular learning styles, focus and conduct learning in particular environments, or learn through problem solving and experimentation. Lastly, some learners wish to be self-reliant by planning, conducting, and demonstrating new learning experiences in their own fashion.

Implications for HRD Professionals: Facilitating Self-Planned Learning

As a professional in human resource development, you are aware of the strengths and the limitations of traditional training models. Although short courses and workshops can be extremely effective and valued, they are labor and resource intensive. In addition, we have come to realize the limitations of prescriptive training packages for our adult learners. We cannot create a learning experience that will be continuously relevant and effective; training workshops and materials have a limited shelf life. Unless adults are continuously engaged in learning experiences, they face a knowledge gap with others who have continued to learn. They face a technology gap with others who seek out and learn new technology. Although training activities are important, they provide limited opportunities for conveying new knowledge to our adult learner clientele. Self-directed learning has become an imperative. Adults in this fast-paced world of new knowledge must be consciously involved in relevant and meaningful learning projects on the job and in their personal lives.

Tough has suggested a new perspective and understanding of adult learning. The metaphor of self-planned learning suggests that we work with adults in their current learning activities and create a different environment and expectation that will support individual learning pursuits. It also suggests that we create organizational awareness, support, and resources for a community of self-planned learning. This book and other works on self-planned, self-directed learning assume that quality learning experiences are anchored in the adult's:

1. *Self-motivation* to learn.
2. *Self-worth* as a learner.
3. *Involvement as a collaborator,* not as a recipient of learning.
4. *Engagement in action and reflection* in the learning experience.
5. *Efforts to design, direct, and evaluate* each learning project.

Thinking Through the Role of Formal Learning

Tough suggests that professional trainers and educators develop new skills in recognizing the broader spectrum of possibilities in adult learning. Adults are more active in self-planned learning than they are in our formal courses, workshops, and training events. When we consider the organization as a learning unit, the majority of adult learning projects occur without our direct intervention and influence. However, we need to realize that most learners are not always efficient and effective independent learners. As designers of a learning environment, we are responsible for creating an organizational learning climate and learning structure that supports, facilitates, and complements the informal, self-planned learning of individual workers. Clearly the role of formal training is important. It provides clear messages and significant learning structures regarding preferred organizational proficiencies and competencies. It also brings together key resources and learning structures for learner access. However, beyond the current programs, workshops, and learning activities of your organization, you must identify the other informal, self-planned learning of individuals and groups in this learning environment.

Rethinking How Adult Workers Learn

Tough suggests several key ideas for professional trainers/educators and educative organizations.

1. *Create learning experiences that reflect the development and use of self-planned learning projects.* Providers of formal training programs should recognize that adult learners enter and exit with learning projects. At the beginning of training programs, we should gather information regarding learner goals and needs, as well as discuss the work context in the specific learning projects. We should not only be concerned about the transfer of training in our workshops, we also should provide support for continued learning through learning projects upon exiting a formal training program. Within the training experience we should incorporate exercises and lecturettes on the nature of self-planned learning. Adults need to be made aware of the conceptualization, design, and implementation of learning projects. We should create an awareness of the significance of these invisible learning activities and their importance to the overall development of the organization.

Adult learners need to understand the empowerment of self-planned learning. As suggested by Tough, most learners need to develop knowledge and skills concerning the identification and utilization of planners. Human resource development professionals may need to reconsider their roles as consultants for goal setting, identification of learning resources and learning strategies, and feedback on learning outcomes. To make self-planned learning more readily available, HRD professionals might consider the development of a library resource room; on-line, resource training data base; expert mentor listing; special network learning groups; and other unique supports and resources.

2. *Reconceptualize the design and implementation of learning experiences.* Self-planned learning suggests an expanded set of assumptions regarding the nature of learning/instruction and of these processes in relation to the outcomes of the learning experience. The HRD professional may find these ideas exciting but may need information and skills to model and implement self-planned learning activities in relation to the organization's training agenda. Tough and other writers would suggest that you begin with an analysis of your own learning and the development of your own self-directed learning knowledge and skills. As facilitators and collaborators in learning projects, we need to develop our knowledge and skills regarding these characteristics and behaviors.

Because of a long tradition of placing value in formal learning systems, HRD professionals should consider how to educate their organizations to this broader perspective and its significance for the future of the organization and its workers. We also need to develop a learning environment that expresses a supportive climate. Because self-planned learning is orchestrated by the learner and may deviate from organizational assumptions, HRD professionals need to determine their ethical involvement and collaboration with adult learners in their organizations. As suggested by Tough, issues of control or expertise are not valid characteristics of a supportive relationship in self-planned learning. Change agents within the organizational setting will need to focus on collaborative relationships; how can they support both the adult learner *and* the work organization in these learning activities? Many HRD consultants have become aware of the broader agenda of learning needs in their organizations. Thus a more global and broad resource support approach has been developed by establishing linkages with other businesses, educational agencies, and human services organizations.

3. *Accept the adventure and risk taking to pursue and create new frameworks, processes, and supports systems.* As Tough suggests, learners will create learning projects and enter into learning experiences based on their current needs, levels of knowledge and skill, and preferences. We, as professional trainers, should enter into this learning relationship based upon the learner's place in the learning path. Our HRD programs and services should be reflective of the diversity of new ideas, needs, and alternative notions supporting self-planned learning. Creating support structures of people and organizational resources becomes imperative. Thus, a responsible freedom for learners to pursue their learning projects and a responsive educational climate to support those learning projects are important in this reframed learning program. As one example, some organizations have created a component in the performance appraisal and development process for workers to focus on their desired, self-planned learning projects for the upcoming year. The organization, at this annual process, aids the worker in refining and prioritizing these learning plans in relation to organizational goals. The organization will commit worker time and resources to support learning plans that will benefit both the worker and the organization. These proposed learning projects are also the catalyst for new training activities, resource allocations toward library and computer network systems in the organization, and creation of new organizational units.

　　　When we consider the driving force of a learning project as the key unit of adult learning, the organization of HRD takes on a new system of possibilities. Many HRD professionals become aware of new ways to create and facilitate a learning environment in the organization. Tough notes the particular value of group support, group inquiry, and a learning network group. Creating these affinity groupings is a particularly creative and powerful effort for the members of a HRD department.

4. *Rethinking evaluation and assessment strategies.* Self-planned learning suggests that a person's competence may be developed both within formal classroom settings as well as in informal, self-planned learning settings. Thus, assessment/evaluation of competence may reflect methods that verify gained knowledge and skill in prescriptive and predefined ways, or methods that verify self-planned and self-conducted learning experiences that rely on more innovative approaches. Self-directed learning places a new twist on our past assumptions of assessment and outcomes. In particular, it suggests that we should consider a

variety of options for an individual to learn a particular competency. Tough suggests that learners will create uniquely different learning projects and learning paths when targeting a
particular learning goal or competency. If we are clear and specific with our learners regarding the desired competency and the
rationale for that competency, Tough suggests that our learners
may be more proficient, involved, and more demanding of
themselves in their learning throughout a learning project than
they will be in a pre-designed training program.

5.   *Focusing on the learner.* In our role as facilitators to adult learn-
     ers, we provide invaluable resources. Tough suggests a number
     of key areas of difficulty for adults in relation to self-planned
     learning:

     a.   Lack of awareness regarding their own learning.
     b.   Inability to visualize or conceptualize the entire learning
          process.
     c.   Difficulty in identifying resources and helpers.
     d.   Denial of need for assistance.
     e.   Inability to access or use the resource.
     f.   Difficulty in identifying resources or strategies to validate or
          gain evaluative feedback on the learned experience.

     In each of these areas, Tough believes that you and your
     HRD unit can have a primary impact. You can aid the adult
     learner to develop greater competence in the design, planning,
     implementation, and impact of the learning project. In essence,
     you can aid each of the workers in your organization to be more
     effective and successful as learners and therefore as workers.

Conclusion

The basic premise of self-directed learning is the belief that adults
do create and engage in their own learning experiences. This belief
does not exclude the HRD professional or pre-designed learning experiences. Rather, Tough suggests that trainers rethink their roles, their
responsibilities, and their impact within this process of self-planned
learning. We need to assist adult learners in becoming more proficient and effective in their own learning process. We also need to
rethink our role and our importance in this process of training and
human development. As suggested by a Chinese proverb, we have
greater impact when we provide the learner with the tools to conduct
effective learning projects over the lifespan, as opposed to providing a

one-shot, packaged learning experience of knowledge that will be obsolete in the future. The challenge and opportunities are evident. Tough's work provides a beginning as you contemplate and create new roles in facilitating self-directed learning for yourself, your organization, and your workers.

References

Tough, A. (1967). *Learning without a teacher: A study of tasks and assistance during adult self-teaching projects.* Toronto, Ontario: Ontario Institute for Studies in Education. (Also available as ERIC Document No. ED 025 688).

Tough, A. (1979). *The adult's learning projects: A fresh approach to theory and practice in adult learning* (2nd ed.). Austin, TX: Learning Concepts.

Tough, A. (1982). *Intentional changes: A fresh approach to helping people change.* Chicago, IL: Follett.

York, D. J. (1991). *Learning in the workplace: Organizational learning climate, self-directed learners and performance at work.* Paper presented at the Fifth International Symposium on Adult Self-directed Learning, University of Oklahoma, Norman, OK.

Chapter Eight

Learning Without a Teacher: A Study of Tasks and Assistance During Adult Self-Teaching Projects

Judith M. O'Donnell on Allen Tough

Dr. O'Donnell is Vice President of O'Donnell & Associates, a management consulting and training organization. She has published several articles in the area of self-directed learning, most recently studying how HRD professionals assess the quality of their work-related, self-directed learning. She has also authored articles on training for performance appraisals and on the use of focus groups for program development and evaluation.

The very title, *Learning Without a Teacher,* has to capture the imagination of every training and development professional. The trainer in a true, helping relationship wants to become less and less important to the trainee, finally working out of the teacher/trainer role to a significant extent. Our guiding proverb might well be: If a man comes to you hungry, you may give him a fish and feed him today. Or you may teach him to fish and feed him a lifetime. Basically, the professional mission in human resource development (HRD) is to help employees reach their full potential through enhancing their unique, individual abilities. Therefore, the goal is to help the learner maintain autonomous responsibility for learning, growth, and problem solving. Toward this end, there has been a continuing fascination with adults as self-directed learners and how we might tap into their learning in order to help them progress.

The purpose of the Tough study was to investigate the self-teaching behavior of adults. Tough defined self-teaching, for this particular study, as any learning episode where the individual acts as the teacher, therefore assuming the responsibility for planning, initiating, and conducting the learning project. One important implication of the research is that by studying the process of learning in the natural environment of everyday life, we can gain significant insight into ways to help adults achieve their learning goals.

Basically, three major questions guided the Tough study:

1. What does the adult do during a self-teaching project? That is, what tasks are central to self-teaching?
2. What areas of self-teaching cause problems and in what ways?
3. How much assistance do self-teachers obtain with their teaching tasks?

The purpose of this chapter is to present an overview of the Tough research. The chapter will first focus on what led Tough to become interested in the self-teaching behavior of adults. This historical perspective is followed by a discussion of the Tough research outline with emphasis on how the study was put together. The research findings and general conclusions will then be reviewed, including a synopsis of the contributions of the work to the field of adult education. The chapter concludes with a discussion of the relationship of this research to the field of human resource development, with some recommendations for action.

Historical Perspective

Have you ever wondered how a person got involved in a particular research topic? Where did the concept or idea originate? What prompts an individual to conduct a particular research study is sometimes as interesting as the research itself.

Allen Tough was a graduate student at the University of Chicago. It was January, 1963, when Professor Cyril O. Houle gave the assignment to his graduate students that would spark Tough's imagination and lead to a research study that would become a classic in the field of adult education. Professor Houle had developed a list of what he considered were fundamental steps in program development. The students were to analyze and describe the way in which the steps had been used in the development of one educational program. Allen Tough chose to apply the model to a self-teaching project he had just completed, namely, an intensive five-week preparation for his comprehensive Ph.D. French exam. Without being aware of consciously following any model, Tough discovered he had accomplished most of the fundamental steps of program development in his own self-teaching.

In 1964, with this discovery still intriguing him, Tough developed his Ph.D. dissertation research on the teaching tasks performed by adults during self-teaching. His research method was as simple as his own initial self-discovery: ask people what they do and how they do it.

The Tough research is a classic for a number of reasons. Foremost, it exemplifies how educational concepts develop. Professor Houle was interested in the elements of program planning. Tough expanded this to the person learning without a teacher by asking how he/she went about conducting the tasks of the learning project. The Tough research is also considered classic because it established a research method that could be duplicated by other researchers. Numerous studies followed (see Caffarella & O'Donnell, 1987, reviewed in Chapter 12 of this book) in which researchers asked what people study, who the self-directed learners are, why they study on their own, what they think about their self-directed learning, and so on.

Learning Without a Teacher is a condensed and modified version of Tough's dissertation. It was first published in 1967. The 1981 edition contains an updated bibliographic guide to more recent books and research.

The Research Outline

The major focus of the study was to investigate the behavior of adults when they had the primary responsibility for planning and conducting a personal learning project. Information was obtained from 40 adults who had engaged in a self-teaching project during the previous year. In an interview format the self-teachers were asked to recall aspects of their behavior and to complete several questionnaires. Tough set up certain criteria for selecting the individuals to take part in the study. One criteria was that the respondents have a college degree. This was selected because Tough believed these individuals would be better able to express their self-teaching activities. Another related criteria was to set a minimum age limit at 21. Finally, in terms of occupation, the researcher simply looked for diversity. All of the subjects chosen for the study were from metropolitan Toronto, Ontario and no attempt was made to interview only people who were adept self-teachers. They simply had to have completed a learning project within the previous year. Needless to say, no generalizations could be made to other populations based on this study.

In order to conduct the investigation, four major areas were addressed prior to beginning the interviews: (1) a definition of self-teaching was developed; (2) a set of 12 major teaching tasks was developed to use as a framework; (3) a classification scheme was developed for the types of people from whom self-teachers obtain assistance; and (4) an interview schedule and questionnaires were developed, tested, and refined. These four areas are presented in more detail below.

Self-Teaching Definition

Though there is a profusion of terms used today to refer to self-directed learning or self-instruction, Tough's research conceptualized the process as self-teaching. Self-teaching was defined as an adult's deliberate and personal attempt to learn some specific knowledge or skill. In this study Tough set out two specific criteria for what would constitute a self-teaching project: (1) the adult learner must have spent at least seven hours on the project and (2) the adult learner, not a professional teacher or organization, must have assumed the primary responsibility for planning, controlling, and supervising the project.

The seven-hour criteria was specified in order to eliminate projects that were not important to the learner. Also, because the learner would be asked to recall specific details, the project would need to have been of long enough duration to provide description and allow the recall.

The criteria of assuming primary responsibility does not mean that the adult learner may not have made use of a professional teacher. Tough maintains that the difference is that the control resides in the learner and not in someone else.

Twelve Teaching Tasks

The research attempted to ascertain what adults do during self-teaching. In order to investigate this behavior, a framework of 12 teaching tasks was developed. These tasks contained a decision or required action by the self-teacher and arose from research into the behavior of classroom teachers. Descriptions of these tasks were revised several times. The goal was to produce a simple yet precise description so that the self-teachers could look at it, assess its relevance to their own project, and be able to articulate whether certain tasks caused any difficulty or concern. These descriptions are paraphrased below.

1. *Decide about a suitable place for learning.* The adult learner may perform the task of deciding in what place learning will occur or may take some action to secure a quiet or otherwise suitable place.

2. *Consider or obtain money for the project.* The adult learner may make a decision of how much money to spend on the project or may take some action to obtain enough money to fund the project.

3. *Decide when to learn and for how long a period.* The adult learner may set one or many deadlines for the project.

4. *Choose the learning goal.* The adult learner may set a general or specific learning goal for the project.

5. *Decide how to achieve the learning goal.* The adult learner may decide how to achieve the goal, what activities to perform, or what needs to be changed in order to achieve the goal.

6. *Obtain or reach people, books, or other resources.* The adult learner may obtain the physical resources necessary for the project, or make the plans to visit or talk with the human resources.

7. *Deal with any lack of desire to finish the project.* The adult learner may try to increase motivation or enthusiasm in a number of ways to realize goal achievement.

8. *Deal with any dislike of necessary activities.* The adult learner may not like the kind or amount of reading or practicing but may take some action to make the learning more interesting or may simply force the concentration and hard work.

9. *Deal with doubts about success.* The adult learner may have to deal with feelings of inadequacy or the fact that the goal may not be reached.

10. *Estimate level of knowledge and skill.* The adult learner may estimate the knowledge and skill achieved or estimate closeness to desired goal.

11. *Deal with difficulty in understanding some parts of the project.* The adult learner may have to deal with the problem of not being able to understand some things or the inability to perform some tasks at first.

12. *Decide whether to continue after reaching a goal.* The adult learner may consider and decide what to do as the next step. The learner may decide to strive for a higher level, move to a related area, or stop the project entirely.

Classification of Assistance Obtained

The very terms we use, self-directed learner or self-teacher, suggest that the learner is isolated from others. This is not the case, however. Tough discovered through preliminary interviews that self-teachers obtain assistance from several people and that this would be an important consideration in any analysis of the behavior of self-teachers.

"There is at least one practical reason for the importance of this aspect: if adult educators are interested in training and assisting self-teachers, they must understand their need for assistance" (Tough, 1981, p. 30).

The classification scheme was developed after an examination of literature, discussion with experts, and exploratory interviews. Seven types of people who provide assistance to the self-teacher were identified. These are described below.

1. *Intimates.* Parents, spouse, close relatives, and two or three close friends.
2. *Librarians.* Includes librarians who were not intimates.
3. *Sales people.* Includes sales people in book stores and/or equipment stores who did not fit into another category.
4. *Fellow learners.* Includes the people trying to learn the same sort of knowledge and skill who did not fit into another category.
5. *Acquaintances.* Includes all friends, relatives, colleagues, and all other people who were not expert in the knowledge and skills being learned and who did not fit into another category.
6. *Experts/personal relationship.* Includes those people who were approached because of a personal relationship, friends, relatives, and colleagues who were experts and who did not fit into another category.
7. *Experts/professional relationship.* Includes those people who were approached on a business or professional relationship who were not friends or relatives and who did not fit into another category.

At first glance the classification scheme may seem lengthy or even redundant. However, reduced to basics, the learners' friends, neighbors, and relatives were divided into those who were especially close (intimates) and those who were not (acquaintances). Subject matter experts were divided into those who were approached primarily because of a personal relationship and those who were not. The two other categories included were librarians and fellow learners.

Interview Schedule and Questionnaires

The 40 subjects were presented with the definition of self-teaching and a list of common self-teaching projects. They were then asked to indicate their own self-teaching activities. Prompting and probing occurred to help each self-teacher to remember learning projects that he/she had conducted and to use the definition to select the one project to use for the interview. The interviewer then asked the subject to list all the individuals who gave assistance with the subject's effort to learn. When this list was completed, the subject was given another list of possible helpers to stimulate recall of as many individuals as possible. These individuals were then classified according to the scheme described in the previous section.

One at a time, the 12 teaching tasks were given to the subject with a questionnaire consisting of five questions:

1. How many times did you consider or perform this task?
2. How much time did you and others spend on all parts of this task?
3. Was any part of this task especially difficult or caused you worry or concern?
4. To what extent did other people help you perform this task?
5. Would you have liked more assistance with this task?

A second questionnaire was used with each task. In this document the subjects used their list of people who helped with the overall project and stated whether they helped with this particular task.

Research Findings and Conclusions

The Tough research found that self-teachers do perform several of the same tasks as the professional teacher. All 40 of the adult self-teachers were found to have performed at least six of the teaching tasks, while the median number of tasks was nine.

Looking at the details of the findings and conclusions, we must acknowledge the three limitations that Tough points out:

1. The 40 subjects were not selected to be representative of some clearly defined population, and so the results cannot be generalized to other populations.
2. The data collection was limited to what the subjects were able to recall and to what they were willing to reveal. Some controversy exists regarding possible interviewer bias using the prompt and probe technique.
3. The findings and conclusions are limited to the 12 teaching tasks used in the study. Different tasks could possibly have produced different results. Also, a very time-consuming and difficult part of any learning project is the performance of the activity, such as reading, practicing, and so on. This was not included in the 12 tasks because it was not a teaching task but a learning task. The hypothesis of the Tough study was that self-teachers do perform

the same tasks as the professional teacher. The data do support this hypothesis for this particular audience.

The Tough research showed that the two most commonly used tasks performed were deciding on activities to reach their learning goals and obtaining resources. All 40 subjects performed these tasks. The least commonly used task was dealing with a lack of desire; however, this task was still performed by 17 of the 40 subjects.

The most time-consuming task for the subjects in the Tough study was estimating their level of knowledge and skill. This task was performed by 31 of the 40 subjects, 10 times or more or even continuously. Deciding on activities, obtaining resources, and deciding about time were also in the top four of the time-consuming tasks. The least time-consuming tasks for the respondents in the study were dealing with a lack of desire and deciding about money.

Every task caused difficulty for some of the self-teachers in the Tough research. However, 17 out of the 40 subjects listed "deciding on learning activities" as one of the two most troublesome; 16 out of 40 listed "dealing with difficult parts of the subject matter" as one of the two most troublesome tasks. "Choosing the goal" and "deciding about money" were the two least troublesome tasks for these self-teachers.

While conducting their self-teaching project, the subjects received assistance from a mean of 10.6 people. Every subject in the study used at least four helpers. The most frequently used helpers were acquaintances and intimates; librarians and fellow learners were the least used helpers. Even for the lowest task on the list, deciding whether to continue with the project, the subjects used a mean of three assistants. Interestingly, each self-teacher used at least one assistant who was not an expert.

The majority of the subjects would have liked more assistance with one, two, or even three tasks. Not surprising, 18 of the 40 subjects would have liked more help with deciding on learning activities; while 14 respondents wanted more help with grasping difficult parts of the subject matter.

In general, the conclusions from the Tough study were that self-teachers perform many of the same tasks that a professional teacher would perform. Each of the 12 tasks included in the study was performed during some phase of the self-teaching project. Most of the self-teachers experienced difficulty or were concerned with at least three of the tasks performed. Only six of the subjects reported no trouble with any of the tasks. Self-teachers in the Tough study received an astonishing amount of assistance with their self-teaching projects. Every subject received help from at least four individuals;

while nearly every subject received help from at least one intimate (immediate family or very close friend) and one acquaintance (friend, relative, or non-expert colleague). Even with all the assistance received, most subjects would have liked more help with at least one or two tasks.

The contributions of this research to the field of adult education are indeed significant. The Tough research gave us new levels of understanding in terms of what self-teachers do and how they do it. It showed us that even sophisticated, college educated people needed probing and prompting in order to classify what they do on their own in terms of learning. Somehow the belief that true or legitimate learning needs an external agent or educational institution had become ingrained. The experiences of the 40 subjects in the Tough research showed that the adult was definitely able to teach him/herself.

The Tough model became the basis for numerous studies that have verified the existence of self-directed learning in very specific populations. Tough provided the research framework for gaining insight into the activities, problems, and feelings of the self-teacher. His highly-structured interview schedules, though criticized by some, were what allowed the replication of the study with diverse groups.

Tough opened the eyes of the adult educator by being able to document the large amount of assistance and number of individuals giving assistance to the self-teachers in his study. The self-directed learner was pretty much ignored at that point in our history. Even more surprising and interesting was the fact that the self-teachers wanted more help with certain tasks. In summary then, Tough was able to show in a limited population study that self-teaching or self-directed learning does not occur in isolation. An important implication was that the area of finding and selecting resources might well be the key entry point for the adult learning professional.

Relationship to Human Resource Development

The Tough research, along with the many verification studies that followed, has much to offer the HRD professional. It is clear from his research that adults engage in self-directed learning and that they would like assistance with their projects. We need to seek the methods whereby we can help adults design, conduct, and evaluate their learning projects. This may well be the most creative assignment faced by the training staff.

First, however, we need to face the problem that Tough pointed out to us. Namely, that we all seem to have fostered the belief that only formal education or formal training is good or acceptable from a learning standpoint. The Tough research method has been criticized because of its use of the probe and prompt technique. The rationale for the criticism is that this technique puts ideas in people's minds and could well slant the research. However, it is easy to see why the technique was used. Test it for yourself by asking someone to tell you about something they have learned during the past year but not anything they learned by attending a course. Even if they come up with something, they will most likely qualify it with comments such as "but it wasn't much" or "it didn't take a lot of brain power." This might be especially true for the workplace learner who has been the recipient of highly-structured, behaviorally-oriented training programs. We need to convince adult learners that learning without a teacher is just as good as learning with a teacher and that it does not have to take place in a specific setting to make it worthwhile. As Tough asks (1981, p. 76), "What is the difference . . . between being taught to swim by a professional swimming teacher and learning from a friend who is an expert swimmer?"

The implications for the HRD professional is to emphasize that self-teaching is an effective way to learn something. Self-teachers with diverse backgrounds and interests can be publicized in company newsletters. Seeing that other people engage in self-directed learning and that the professionals in the training department think it is good might, in time, reduce the feeling in some adults that what we learn on our own is inferior.

Training could be given on goal setting to reduce the problems that some self-teachers appear to have with that task. Training in selecting resources and how to use and benefit from different resources (including practice time) may also be beneficial for the adult learners.

The human resource department could become a clearinghouse for resources, for study groups, and for resident experts to share their personal learning projects during brown bag lunches. Self-learners could also be given help on ways to evaluate learning. The sky is the limit in terms of providing materials, videos, and people resources for the adult who wants to learn without a teacher. With management's support and backing, the HRD department could allow new managers the freedom to teach themselves how to conduct performance appraisals, how to discipline employees, or the how's and why's of delegating.

This certainly goes beyond our current self-paced or programmed instruction where one course fits all learners. It is definitely more work to remain flexible and to help the learner find what he wants to know. The results, however, from maintaining this flexibility could be very far reaching. By helping the individual learn to learn without a teacher, we are, in effect, giving employees the tools to solve today's problems and tomorrow's problems as well.

Summary

Allen Tough studied the self-teaching behavior of 40 adults in Toronto. In answer to the question, "What does an adult do during self-teaching?" he found that these adults performed many of the same teaching tasks a professional educator would perform. In answer to the question, "Which aspects of self-teaching cause difficulty and concern?" he found that deciding on learning activities was the most troublesome. The learners in the Tough study expressed having trouble with deciding what to read or whom to talk with or how to achieve their learning goal. Dealing with difficult parts of the subject matter was also troublesome to the respondents in this study. In answer to the question, "How much assistance do self-teachers obtain with each of the teaching tasks?" the answer was, "An astonishing amount of help." Overall, every subject in the study used at least four assistants. These same respondents suggested that more help was needed, especially in the two troublesome areas mentioned above.

The Tough research was a classic in the field of adult education because it showed learning within the natural environment of everyday life, showed a role for the adult educator in helping the adult self-learner, and was easily duplicated in other studies so as to further our knowledge base. Some ideas for using the findings within a HRD department were given. Primarily, the training professional was challenged to develop creative ways to tap into the self-directed nature of the adult learner and to become the resource clearinghouse for work-related, self-teaching projects.

References

Caffarella, R., & O'Donnell, J. M. (1987). Self-directed learning: A critical paradigm revisited. *Adult Education Quarterly, 37*(4), 199-211.

Tough, A. M. (1981). *Learning without a teacher: A study of tasks and assistance during adult self-teaching projects.* Toronto, Ontario: The Ontario Institute for Studies in Education.

Chapter Nine

The Organizing Circumstance: Environmental Determinants in Self-Directed Learning

Russell F. West on Geroge E. Spear and Donald Mocker

Dr. West is Associate Professor of Educational Leadership and Policy Analysis at East Tennessee State University. He has conducted research into the self-directed learning efforts of medical students and public school teachers. Dr. West has also studied the quality of instruments commonly used to assess self-directed learning. He teaches courses related to adult learning and research methodology.

Are self-directed learners effective educational planners? Is the process of self-directed learning regular and orderly? Is there an identifiable sequence of steps that adult learners follow when they engage in self-directed learning? What role does the environment or life circumstance play in shaping the nature and character of adult learning? These were some of the major questions asked by George Spear and Donald Mocker as they studied the learning efforts of 78 self-directed learners who had completed less than a high school education. In studying these learners Spear and Mocker identified the importance of environmental or life circumstances in structuring the learning of these adults. Their research highlighted the impact that workplace structure can have on the self-directed learning efforts of employees.

Background and Context for the Study

In 1981, George Spear and Donald Mocker reported on their recently completed study (in association with Kirschner Associates, Inc.) on the learning activities of adults with less than a twelfth-grade education (Spear & Mocker, 1981). As first conceived, their original study of formal and non-formal learning was very much like the early studies on adults' learning projects, which grew out of the initial work of Allen Tough (See Chapter 7). In their initial study Spear and Mocker were very interested in determining the type of learning projects adults were pursuing. In addition, they had expected to identify the steps adults followed as they planned their learning projects. These expectations were based on earlier studies that revealed the pervasiveness of self-directed learning among different adult populations (e.g., Tough, 1971; Tough, 1978). In addition, Tough (1971) and Knowles (1975) had suggested that self-directed learning projects emerged out of a very logical planning process. For example, Tough (1971) had identified a thirteen-step planning process that included such activities as deciding on the knowledge and skill to be learned, deciding on activities or resources, deciding where to learn, setting goals, deciding when to learn, and deciding on the pace. Knowles (1975) also published his brief paperback book titled *Self-Directed Learning: A Guide for Learners and Teachers* in which the competencies underlying self-directed learning were identified. In these writings and in other prior studies, the learner had been predominantly portrayed as a deliberate decision-maker faced with many alternatives as he or she engaged in self-directed learning. The literature on self-directed learning had, up until the work of Spear and Mocker, painted a picture of the self-directed learner as a purposeful and orderly planner who knew what he or she needed to learn and who could chose the "best" sequence of steps to meet his or her learning goals.

The Initial Focus of Spear and Mocker

Spear and Mocker began their initial study of self-directed learners with the expectation of confirming the existence of this deliberate planning process, a process that looked something like the linear process a teacher would follow in planning instruction for others in a traditional classroom setting. *In The Organizing Circumstance: Environmental Determinants in Self-Directed Learning* (1984), Spear and Mocker noted:

> This study was expected to confirm the presence of such a planning process in the self-directed learning experience of the participants, and the interview schedule included a series of direct questions intended to reveal that process (p. 3).

The purpose of the original study was to compare the experience of adults who where engaged in formal educational activities (activities organized and conducted by some organization or agency) and those who were engaged in self-directed learning (activities controlled primarily by the learner in alternative settings). The sample consisted of 158 adults who had not completed a twelfth-grade education or equivalent. These respondents were from Miami, Florida; Chicago, Illinois; Washington, D. C.; Kansas City, Missouri; and San Diego, California. While there were a total of 158 learners in the overall study, the researchers focused their analysis on the 78 adults who had reported engaging in self-directed learning efforts.

Utilizing a New Method of Assessing Self-Directed Learning

In addition to employing data collection procedures similar to those used in many previous studies of self-directed learning, Spear and Mocker used open-ended questions with these learners, asking them to describe exactly how they went about learning. In the analysis they tried to identify why these adults became involved in their learning efforts and what took place as they learned. This represented a departure from previous research on self-directed learning because they were able to obtain a rich description of the dynamics of the learning process. According to Spear and Mocker (1984):

> The analysis centered initially on the motivating force or triggering event that set the process in motion. Further, the analyses were directed primarily to why and how decisions regarding the learning process were made. These foci tended to differ from previous research, which had emphasized what resources were used, how much time was spent learning, how many projects were conducted, and where learning took place (p. 2).

Spear and Mocker clearly felt that they were moving beyond what Caffarella and O'Donnell (1987) called the "verification" studies of self-directed learning; i.e., those studies in which the number of projects, areas of study, and types of resources used were inventoried.

As Spear and Mocker began the initial analysis of the data, they were surprised to find very little evidence to support the argument that self-directed learners go through a deliberate process in planning their learning. The researchers noted that "throughout the study, evidence of preplanning did not occur, except in rare instances and then in only vague fashion" (p. 3). For the researchers the mystery in this initial data analysis phase was the discovery that:

At the same time, it was noted that, although self-directed learners apparently did not do detailed preplanning . . . Indeed, there was evidence of definite order, deliberateness and logic in the process (p. 3).

Taking a Second Look at the Data

Out of the apparent inconsistency in these early findings, Spear and Mocker began to analyze the interviews differently, using a secondary analysis approach. They went back to the original interview results and began to ask different questions and to look at the data differently. The researchers tried to answer the puzzling question: How were these adults able to engage in learning when they were not fully aware of what they were supposed to learn and had no real learning plan?

The Major Findings

In marked contrast to the previous research on self-directed learning, Spear and Mocker found that learners with less than a twelfth-grade education were not faced with a large number of decisions when engaged in self-directed learning because their range of choice was very limited. In most cases, decision making was minimized in terms of which resources to use, when to learn, and where to learn. In other words, the environmental circumstances surrounding the learners provided the structure in which learning occurred. For example, in occupationally-oriented learning, the workplace frequently determined the type and quality of learning that occurred.

The researchers explained this deviation from previous research by suggesting that while a logical preplanning process may occur in the learning efforts of those with a high degree of exposure to formalized education (those with more formal schooling), such a linear planning process does not occur among those unfamiliar with instructional planning models. For adult learners unfamiliar with the notion of curriculum development, learning was not planned but was structured by their environmental circumstance. Spear and Mocker referred to this new concept as the "organizing circumstance." The authors also implied that many of the previous studies on self-directed learning had demonstrated evidence of elaborate planning because of the questions that were asked by the researchers, most of whom were very familiar with curriculum or instructional planning models.

Spear and Mocker suggested that the deliberate planning process did not reflect the experience of those who were unfamiliar with the formal educational process. The researchers central argument and point of departure from previous studies was stated as follows:

> From the above rationale, the researchers derived the concept of the *Organizing Circumstance* which postulates that self-directed learners, rather than pre-planning their learning projects, tend to select a course from limited alternatives which occur fortuitously within their environment, and which structures their learning projects . . . The Organizing Circumstance, rather than preplanning by the individual, is the directing force behind much, perhaps most, self-directed learning for this population (p. 4).

This new concept of organizing circumstance represented a significant departure from previous thinking about the factors that lead to self-directed learning. Much of the prior literature had focused on social or demographic factors associated with self-directed learning. Factors such as age, level of education, or ethnicity were explored in previous studies as possible antecedents to self-directed learning. Spear and Mocker challenged this thinking by suggesting it was the environment and its arrangement that led to self-directed learning. They suggested that by arranging the environment one could facilitate self-directed learning and argued that the organizing circumstance was more important in determining participation in self-directed learning than demographic or socioeconomic characteristics.

Environmental Influences in Self-Directed Learning

As a result of analyzing each of the interviews, Spear and Mocker generated a set of statements that reflected the general process of self-directed learning among the learners they studied. This process is outlined in figure 9.1.

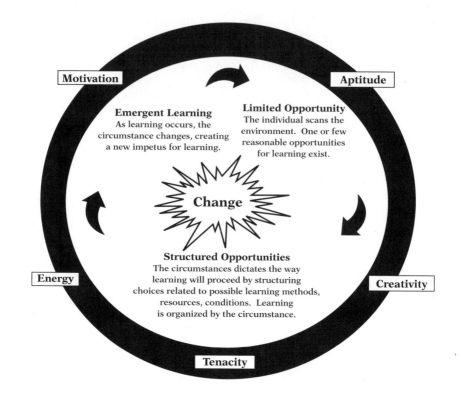

Figure 9.1 A summary of the learning process identified by George Spear and Donald Mocker.

As shown in the model, Spear and Mocker suggested that nearly all self-directed learning was initiated by some change that occurred in the individual's environment. The change did not necessarily have to affect the learner directly, because it could be based on an observation of others. For example, an electronics technician working in an industrial establishment may recognize that several co-workers were promoted because they learned to run a new piece of computerized equipment. While this change may not directly affect the worker, this event could serve as the impetus for his or her learning how to operate the machinery.

In addition to the impetus for change, the researchers identified a scan of the environment in which the learners looked for possible opportunities. Spear and Mocker found that typically one or only a few reasonable or attractive learning opportunities existed for the individuals. Spear and Mocker interviewed only those who *had* engaged in learning. The findings suggest, however, that much learning potential can be lost at this point simply because no opportunities are available in the environment. Consider the situation of the medical technologist who realizes that his "bench techniques" are not effective after he was recently cited on two occasions for improperly crossmatching blood types. The impetus for learning may be strong, but unless some opportunity for learning exists in the environment, unless the hospital provides some guidance or structure, learning will not occur and the individual will not grow or develop. From a human resource development standpoint, it is critical that the organization create the circumstance that facilitates the development of the employee.

In direct contrast to those who previously discussed self-directed learning as a process of selecting from many available alternatives, Spear and Mocker found that most often the individual did not have much control over the nature of the learning experience. Methods of learning, available resources, and the conditions under which learning occurred were to a great extent determined by the environment, and individual choice was limited.

Finally, the authors found that as an individual learned, his or her conditions changed. This changed circumstance often resulted in new opportunities for learning, the availability of new resources, different conditions for learning, and a new set of learning needs. Rather than viewing self-directed learning as a linear or step-by-step process, Spear and Mocker suggested that the impetus and opportunity for learning was emergent, growing out of prior learning and experience. Learning was viewed as a continuous process of change.

Spear and Mocker also found that each circumstance was different because individuals had their own unique personal attributes, including motivations, aptitudes, energy, creativity and tenacity, which shaped the way they interacted with the environment. They postulated that no two individuals would experience a given circumstance in the same way because of these unique individual characteristics.

This idea of continually changing conditions and emergent learning can be illustrated by the case of a young man who works in the stockroom of a self-service discount store. He is the father of a new son. As a result of this new situation, he recognizes a need to learn more about the stockroom and its operation so that he might move into a position that pays a higher salary. The young man begins to watch his immediate supervisor who is responsible for inventory control and begins to work closely with him as an informal inventory apprentice. Over time the young man learns to perform in this capacity, and as a result of a change in personnel, the young man is promoted to a supervisory level. This change to a supervisory position, however, serves as an impetus to develop skills in supervising others and the young man checks out several video-based, management training seminars from the company self-learning library. These changes were not, however, planned out in advance. Rather, each emerged from a prior situation.

The Four Common Types of Circumstances

Spear and Mocker identified four major types of circumstances or patterns that provided the structure for the learning activities of adults with less than a high school education.

Circumstance #1: A New Situation in Which Learning is Expected

Spear and Mocker found adults undertaking new activities or entering new situations where it was assumed or anticipated that some learning would be required. These individuals did not know how this learning would occur or what should be learned. They expected or relied on the new circumstance to provide the structure for this learning effort. These individuals had confidence that the situation would provide this structure for them and recognized that learning would be necessary. These learners were willing and able to learn. This type of circumstance reflects the type of assistance often offered to new employees or employees new to a particular job.

As an example of this type of organizing circumstance, consider the new worker hired to take phone orders for a large, retail company. The employee has had no prior experience taking phone orders and has never used a computer terminal. She does, however, want to learn the job and has confidence that the company will show her the way. Prior to beginning the job, she watches a computerized video program on the company and the order-taking process. She then works through a simulated order-taking program in the training department and receives feedback on her performance. She takes written material home to read and is able to watch and talk with others who are performing on the job. Finally, she feels that she has learned the skills necessary to perform effectively. The company has done its part in helping her structure her learning by making the learning resources and time available to her.

Circumstance #2: A New or Different Situation Where Learning is Not Expected

Spear and Mocker found that many individuals entered new situations or activities in which there was no expectation that learning would occur. Rather, through observation, individuals developed an awareness of the knowledge and skills necessary to perform. Some of those individuals even practiced some of the skills individually. Under these circumstances learning was an unintended by-product.

Consider the case of a kitchen worker who is hired to wash dishes in the hospital cafeteria. The worker has had no experience in the food service industry and is unfamiliar with the equipment and work processes. The worker works beside the cafeteria cooks, however. Over time he watches the cooks utilize their work skills to run the kitchen equipment and prepare the food. As he observes, he notes the specific tasks that must be performed. Occasionally he will ask or be asked to run a piece of equipment or perform a food processing procedure. Eventually he may ask to perform some of the duties of a cook. On special occasions he is allowed to cook and works to perfect his skills when those opportunities develop. In this case the employee has learned to cook. He took the kitchen helper job, however, without an intention of learning. His learning has been structured by the kinds of equipment that are used and the type of food produced in this organization. Learning is a by-product of the circumstance because the kitchen worker was not expected to be engaged in learning and did not expect to do so. In a sense he was in the right place at the right time.

Circumstance #3: A Series of Learning Events in Which One Event is Related to the One that Follows It

According to Spear and Mocker, some adults engage in a series of several learning efforts that are related to one another in some way, yet the process is not linear. Rather each learning effort grows out of the one that preceded it. These learning events may be spread out over a long period of time. Each time learning occurs the circumstance changes, at least to some degree. This new circumstance changes the situation and influences future learning.

An example of this type of organizing circumstance can be seen in the learning of a garment manufacturing plant laborer who learned to operate a sewing machine through observation in the plant. By filling in on an occasional basis, he learned about the different types of machines and the parts associated with each one. Over time he began to watch and work with the sewing machine repairer, often working with the repairer on his own time and learning how to fix the machines. Eventually he was promoted to the job of machine repairer where he worked more closely with the plant manager. Finally, his growing association with the plant office, combined with a detailed knowledge of plant operations and understanding of the employees, earned him the title of general plant supervisor, where his new responsibilities included direct supervision of workers.

In retrospect these different periods of learning appear to be completely planned in advanced, yet Spear and Mocker found that most of the time such sequences are not planned in advance. Rather each event creates a new situation that calls for additional learning. A key element in this type of circumstance is the opportunity the employee has to learn from others in the organization. What appears to be a linear process on the exterior is really a connected series of learning efforts that are not all directed toward a final outcome or goal.

Circumstance #4: A Series of Unrelated Learning Events

According to Spear and Mocker, the fourth type of organizing circumstance occurs over a long period of time and as a result of many life experiences. Hence this can be considered a culminating circumstance. As adults move through the life cycle they collect what at the time appear to be random pieces of information or observations. These bits of information and perceptions are stored in memory. At some later time, when confronted with a changing situation, this information may suddenly be recalled and act as the organizing factor. Many seemingly isolated pieces of information, which represent the individual's "fund of knowledge" (p. 7), may suddenly come together to organize the learning experience.

Consider the example of the medical doctor who has taken a new position as a faculty member in a medical school. In that new role she is asked to engage in a research project with a colleague. The new faculty member's learning is to a large measure structured by the fund of information the individual has about the research process. She had taken a statistics course many years ago in medical school. In her medical practice she developed an awareness of the research problems that were most pressing from the perspective of the practitioner. She also has images of what a research study should look like, based on her experience in reading the popular literature and her sporadic reading of the medical research literature. Finally, she has talked with her medical school colleagues about the publish or perish syndrome that pervades this particular medical school. All of these unrelated pieces of information and perception are brought together to structure the manner in which she approaches the research study.

While these four types or patterns of circumstances were the ones seen most often by Spear and Mocker, other patterns may exist. The identification of these organizing circumstances, along with the previously mentioned findings, suggest several important points that should be considered by human resource development professionals when working with adult learners in the organization.

Implications for Training and Development

The work of George Spear and Donald Mocker and the concept of organizing circumstance provide a unique perspective from which to view the adult learner in the organizational setting. This is a perspective that is quite different from the one proposed out of the earlier studies of self-directed learning.

Perhaps the first and most obvious finding was the pervasiveness of adult self-directed learning among a group of learners who had not completed a high school education. Spear and Mocker found that approximately one-half of the adults surveyed were engaged in self-directed learning projects in such areas as adult basic education, occupational entry, occupational retraining, and occupational maintenance. This finding highlights the importance of self-directed learning to workers at all levels in the organization. It also underscores the critical importance of self-directed learning to workers who are trying to make occupational adjustments. The researchers felt these findings provided evidence that motivation to learn is not the major issue in human resource development. Rather it is a matter of arranging the environment to facilitate learning. Whether an employee is working on the assembly line or in a supervisory position, self-directed learning represents an important and pervasive means of occupational improvement.

One of the major findings of Spear and Mocker was the fact that much of the learning that occurred in the workplace was structured by the environment. Workers very often take a new job or move into a new position within the company, fully expecting that learning will be required. These workers expect to learn things and have a high level of learning readiness. Whether from a lack of familiarity with traditional educational planning, an alienation from educational processes, or other reasons, many of these employees expect the workplace to provide both the content and processes for learning. In the literature on self-directed learning, this finding has led to a great deal of subsequent discussion of what is meant by the term self-directed.

The work of Spear and Mocker suggests that many workers have little understanding of what they need to learn to perform effectively. It is critical that the organization help them identify required learning and available resources, as well as provide the time necessary for learning to occur.

While learning may not be the primary intent of the organization, it is essential to arrange the environment so that the employee will not fail. For example, when working with a new employee, it is critical that a vision of the job be shared. The supervisor might also suggest the type of learning that will be required and the resources available to assist with the learning effort. Finally, time must be provided for the worker/learner to utilize the resources. Often workers are placed in a new work situation and surrounded by resources, yet little time is available to access the resources. Under such constraints the learning quality is diminished along with the motivation for future learning.

These findings also highlighted the importance of providing a variety of resources from which employees can learn. Spear and Mocker found that generally the number of possible resources and formats for learning were very limited for their group of adults with less than a high school education. Individual choice was very limited, yet the employees relied on the workplace to provide this structure. These results suggest that employees cannot always take advantage of the singular options that are available. Given these results and the recent attention to learning style differences among adults, it is critical that human resource development professionals within the workplace offer a variety of learning opportunities that allow the employees to find an effective approach to learning. Given the dependence of employees on the organization, it goes without saying that the quality of workplace learning (and ultimately the quality of the product produced) will be directly related to the quality of resources that are provided for learning.

The findings of Spear and Mocker also underscore the importance of everyday experiences as organizers for future learning in the workplace. Employees learn by watching and interacting with co-workers. They may unintentionally accumulate seemingly random bits of information and develop their perspectives through daily interactions. At some future point, when a conscious decision is made to learn a new task or procedure, these pieces of information will be pulled together to structure learning. An effective organization can capitalize on this tendency of adults to learn through observation and incidental contact, by structuring the workplace and workflow so employees are in contact one another and have the opportunity to see what others are doing. This broad exposure can help employees accumulate these individual pieces of information into a meaningful gestalt that may assist them when called on to move into another work role within the organization.

The findings of this study also indicate the importance of using more experienced co-workers as resources for learning in the workplace. While this is certainly not a new concept, it is often ignored in the workplace. These findings suggest that human resource development professionals should consider the use of experienced mentors with new employees or with employees engaged in job change. Both anticipated and unanticipated learning will increase when this type of interaction is encouraged.

The results also indicate that many individual learning efforts stem from some prior experience and lead to change in an employee's situation, requiring future learning. These individual learning efforts provide a tremendous opportunity to help employees clarify their own occupational needs and interests. Such an employee counseling approach can lead to a more satisfied work force and the discovery of talent within the organization.

Summary

Spear and Mocker found self-directed learning efforts to be common among adults with less than a high school education, yet they found little evidence of planning for those projects. Their concept of the organizing circumstance highlighted the importance of the physical and social aspects of the environment in structuring the learning of adults. The authors felt that previous research had focused too much on a deliberate planning process that was learner controlled. While stressing the importance of environment in providing structure for learning, they also cautioned against discounting the personal attributes of the learner. They suggested that:

> This discussion is not intended to promote a behavioristic or deterministic point of view. It allows for individual autonomy and free will. However, it does contend that choice or free will takes place within an area of circumstances, which, at the same time, provides for but also limits alternatives to actions (p. 9).

Spear and Mocker provided a useful concept in the term "organizing circumstance," which highlighted the tremendous responsibility of the organization in providing for a physical, social, and psychological climate in which self-directed learning can occur. Since its introduction by Spear and Mocker, the concept has generated a great deal of discussion among those with an interest in the field (Garrison, 1989; Spear, 1988; Tremblay & Theil, 1991). Human resource development professionals can capitalize on the development opportunities suggested in these early findings, to bring about quality learning in the workplace and an increase in the creative potential of the organization.

References

Caffarella, R. S., & O'Donnell, J. M. (1987). Self-directed adult learning: A critical paradigm revisited. *Adult Education Quarterly, 37*, 199-211.

Garrison, D. R. (1989). Facilitating self-direction in learning: Not a contradiction in terms. In H. B. Long & Associates, *Self-directed learning: Emerging theory and practice,* (pp. 53-62.) Norman, OK: Oklahoma Research Center for Continuing Professional and Higher Education, University of Oklahoma.

Knowles, M. S. (1975). *Self-directed learning.* NY: Association Press.

Mocker, D. W., & Spear, G. E. (1982). *Lifelong learning: Formal, informal, and self-directed learning.* Kansas City, MO: Center for Resource Development Education. University of Missouri at Kansas City. (ERIC Document Reproduction Service No. ED 220 723).

Spear, G. E., & Mocker, D. W. (1981). *The organizing circumstance: Environmental determinants in self-directed learning.* Kansas City, MO: Center for Resource Development in Adult Education, University of Missouri at Kansas City.

Spear, G. E., & Mocker, D. W. (1984). The organizing circumstance: Environmental determinants in self-directed learning. *Adult Education Quarterly, 35*, 1-10.

Spear, G. E. (1988). Beyond the organizing circumstances: A search for methodology for the study of self-directed learning. In H. B. Long and Associates, *Self-directed learning: Application and theory,* (pp. 199-221). Athens, GA: Adult Education Department, University of Georgia.

Tremblay, N. A., & Theil, J. P. (1991). A conceptual model of autodidactism. In H. B. Long & Associates, *Self-directed learning: Consensus and conflict,* (pp. 29-51). Norman, OK: Oklahoma Research Center for Continuing Professional and Higher Education, University of Oklahoma.

Tough, A. (1971). *The adult's learning projects.* Toronto, Ontario: The Ontario Institute for Studies in Education.

Tough, A. (1978). Major learning efforts: Recent research and future directions. *Adult Education, 28*, 250-263.

Chapter Ten

Self-Directed Learning:
From Theory to Practice

Roger Hiemstra on Stephen Brookfield

Dr. Hiemstra is Professor of Adult Education and Chairperson of the Department of Adult Education at Syracuse University. Long interested in self-directed learning, he has conducted or supervised several research projects related to the topic. He has published several works in the field including, Self-Direction in Adult Learning: Perspectives on Theory, Research and Practice *(1991), which he coauthored with Ralph Brockett. Currently he consults with various groups, helping them individualize instructional and training efforts for adults.*

I had the good fortune to meet and work with Stephen Brookfield fairly early in his career. We both overlapped a few weeks during summer teaching stints at the University of British Columbia in 1981. As we shared common interests in self-directed learning (hereafter referred to as SDL) and finding ways to individualize the instructional process, we discussed research and knowledge stemming from Houle's seminal work (see Chapter 4) and Tough's initial work in the sixties (1966, 1967) that culminated in his 1971 and 1979 publications (see Chapter 7 for this latter one).

It was then that I became aware of Steve's own scholarship stemming from some program development and research experiences in his home country of England (Brookfield, 1978, 1980, 1981a, 1981b). We maintained contact after that summer; I visited him in England once and he visited the Syracuse University campus a couple of times. I was especially pleased, therefore, when he obtained a position at Teachers College (Columbia University) and we could more easily maintain contact.

Steve continued his work with SDL and published important summaries of his thinking in 1982 and 1984 (1984a). During his initial years at Teachers College he helped to develop a non-traditional, doctoral studies program in adult education that incorporated some SDL principles and theory. This program is described later in this chapter. He began to provide some critical analysis of Tough's work (Brookfield, 1981a, 1984a, 1984b) and raised important issues about quality:

> [A] lack of attention to the quality of learning — in terms of some external measure of its effectiveness and the learner's own perception of its usefulness — characterizes much research in this area . . . The emphasis on the amount rather than the effectiveness of independent learning has dominated the research in the field. It is now timely and appropriate, I would suggest, for more attention to be paid to the quality of independent adult learning. (Brookfield, 1984a, p. 46).

In 1984 and 1985 he and Ralph Brockett had a spirited exchange of views about SDL in the *Adult Education Quarterly* (Brockett, 1985; Brookfield, 1985a).

Out of all this ferment and a desire to provide a good overview of available information and thinking regarding the topic, Steve convinced several authors to work together on the product that is this essay's subject. Thus, this chapter's purpose is both to summarize important aspects of that product and to describe ways some of the information can be used in facilitating our work with adult learners.

Conceptualizing a Product

The Jossey-Bass *New Directions Quarterly Sourcebooks* are designed to provide readers with current information on specific topics. Steve conceptualized the *New Directions for Continuing Education Sourcebook Number 25* as a product that would bridge the gap between much of the research related to SDL and the practice that is being or can be benefitted by such research. He wanted to showcase some of the various attempts to work with adults in self-directed modes. Thus, he pulled together a diverse group of authors with varied experiences in studying and promoting self-directed, individualized learning.

The *Sourcebook* is divided into eight chapters. The first section, containing Chapters One through Three, provides an overview of the research and theory associated with SDL and corresponding efforts to bridge the gap between theory and practice. Section two, Chapters Four through Six, presents three case studies of SDL in practice, including an examination of efforts in higher education, cultural institutions, and the health professions. The third section includes Chapters Seven and Eight in which some community-wide SDL services are described and several resources for continual study are outlined, respectively.

A 1985 publication cannot, of course, capture the research, theory building, and thinking that comes after that date. However, this *Sourcebook* does provide a useful reference or starting point for those who desire a fairly concise summary of various aspects of SDL.

A Critical Review of Research

The first chapter of this *Sourcebook* (Brookfield, 1985d) includes a brief history of SDL research. Here Brookfield cautions readers about "accepting uncritically a new academic orthodoxy in adult education" (p. 5). He also attempts to set a tone for the sourcebook and proposes to subject research and theory to a "close and critical scrutiny" (p. 6). Brookfield suggests that SDL researchers and theorists have prompted us to challenge the assumption that adult learning can occur only in the presence of accredited teachers.

He also describes the various social settings in which SDL can occur and talks about the concept in relation to issues like learning style and levels of learner independence. Brookfield urges that a quest to promote critical reflection among adult learners be incorporated into any SDL efforts. He later develops these notions further in another book project (Brookfield, 1989).

Building a Critical Theory of SDL

Jack Mezirow (1985), a faculty colleague of Brookfield's at Teachers College, crafts a chapter that speculates on the purpose, processes, and conditions required for learning that is aimed at building individual awareness. He critically analyzes some commonly held assumptions about learning and describes various implications for educators of adults. For example, he suggests that learning should be classified in different ways:

1. *Instrumental learning* that is observable, deductive in nature, or related to task-oriented, problem-solving efforts.
2. *Dialogic learning* that involves critical understanding of what others mean in communicating with us.

3.   *Self-reflective learning* that involves understanding ourselves and any dependencies or inhibitions potentially affecting our learning abilities.

Mezirow also describes what he refers to as perspective transformation and critical reflectivity, two concepts he had introduced in earlier publications (1975, 1978, 1981) and continued to expand in later works (Mezirow, 1991; Mezirow & Associates, 1991). He suggests that learners should be encouraged to participate in dialogue designed to diagnose their own learning needs.

Bridging the Theory-Practice Gap

Brockett, a professor at the University of Tennessee, and Hiemstra, a professor at Syracuse University (1985), saw their chapter as a mechanism for filtering some of the existing SDL theory and research in order to distill several implications for practice. For example, they describe several teaching strategies, instructor roles, and learning resources related to SDL. Their ideas about facilitating self-directed, individualized learning have been expanded in later publications (Brockett & Hiemstra, 1991; Hiemstra & Sisco, 1990).

Their basic notion is that SDL research has demonstrated the value of adults taking responsibility for their own learning. They describe the weekend scholar program at Syracuse University as one illustration of a programmatic effort to build credit courses around notions of facilitating learners in assuming such responsibility.

They also present several policy recommendations related to SDL for program administrators, instructors, and others to consider. The policies are aimed at adult learners, continuing educators, and agencies that provide educational resources for adults. They also are concerned about several ethical questions that must be asked as educators of adults begin to incorporate SDL principles. For example, "How can quality be maintained when learners assume considerable responsibility for their own learning decisions?"

Self-Directed Learning in a Graduate Program

Bauer (1985) describes the Adult Education Guided Independent Study (AEGIS) program designed for non-traditional doctoral study in adult education at Teachers College, Columbia University. Bauer was the program's administrator in 1985. The mission of the AEGIS program is to assist continuing education practitioners to exercise and further develop their own self-directedness. The program has five primary objectives:

1. To help learners acquire andragogical* perspectives.
2. To transfer responsibility for learning to students.
3. To facilitate for learners the growth of critical reflection and analysis skills.
4. To help learners become aware of the theoretical contexts that undergird problems in adult education.
5. To promote interest and skill in disciplined inquiry.

The chapter includes a description of how the AEGIS program works, including its independent study, pass-fail approach, intensive summer courses, monthly half-day seminars, and mechanisms for communicating with faculty. The first year involves students diagnosing their own learning needs, designing individual learning contracts to guide their future study, building basic knowledge of the adult education field, and building critical analysis skills. The second year involves obtaining some advanced understanding of adult learning and program development, writing critical analysis papers, and preparing for their research. The chapter also describes some of the constraints the program has had to overcome.

Self-Directed Learning in Cultural Institutions

The next chapter by Carr (1985), a Rutgers University professor, describes some SDL possibilities in various cultural institutions. For example, he describes how museums and libraries foster autonomous, individualized learning among adults. In essence learners can make choices on what they study or learn. For instance, in a museum a tool or some object can become an example or an application object for some new learning. In other words, cultural institutions offer an experiential invitation to the self-directed learner that can be both personal and public.

Carr describes the value and importance of forming good questions to guide any learning effort. Some learners will need more help than others in grasping complex information and meanings. Thus adult educators in cultural institutions must learn how to help such

---

*Andragogy, the art and science of helping adults learn, is a concept introduced in the United States by Knowles (1970). The instructional approaches that have been associated with andragogy typically incorporate self-directed learning principles.

learners in their study efforts by providing useful reference tools, opportunities to examine specific specimens, and access to subject specialists.

Applying SDL Principles in the Health Professions

In the last of the three case studies showing SDL in actual practice, Ash (1985) describes some of the responses that have been made to a growing need for SDL in the health professions. The varied and often individualized learning needs of health care workers, the necessity for continuous learning to keep up with constant change in health care, and the busy schedules of many health care workers make SDL a necessity.

Ash describes some examples of how SDL has been applied in the health professions. These include such activities as the following:

1. Establishing learning resource centers.
2. Developing SDL modules on specific topics.
3. Training educators to serve as facilitators of individualized learning.
4. Creating orientation training programs via an individualized learning contract.
5. Finding staff nurses who will serve as preceptors to guide others in individualized learning.

Because of her involvement as director of nursing education at the Memorial Sloan-Kettering Cancer Center in New York City, she describes how much of the training for nurses is based on andragogical principles. In essence, they assume that nurses are professionals who are capable of SDL, and such learning is fostered and encouraged. She also identified some of the problems that can be encountered, such as student hesitancy, learner frustration, extra space requirements for individualized modules and associated equipment, and the difficulties that can be encountered in evaluating learning or training faculty who will support SDL.

The Continuing Educator's Support of SDL in the Community

Brookfield (1985c) in this chapter describes some examples of how SDL can be supported in a community. He uses as a base for his discussion his work in an English community in the mid to late seventies. There he participated in the gathering of information about local community groups to determine what kind of learning was already occurring and what kinds of settings for learning existed.

In responding to some of the knowledge that was obtained, he assisted in the development of an educational advisory service for adults. This advisory service provided some support for adults seeking various educational opportunities in the community and facilitated self-directed learning efforts. Another opportunity provided to learners was a home study service where learners were assisted in diagnosing needs and designing an appropriate learning contract of future study efforts. Tutorials, courses, weekend workshops, and supporting autonomous adult learning groups were some other services developed to meet the adult learners' needs.

Self-Directed Learning Theory and Practice Resources

As is common with most *New Directions Sourcebooks*, Brookfield (1985b) provides annotated descriptions of various sources for further study. Most of the 15 sources chosen for this chapter still retain much value. Three of the references are related to research on SDL, and the remainder are devoted to actual practice where aspects of self-directed, individualized learning are described or employed.

Contributions to our Work with Adult Learners

Brookfield's *Sourcebook* involved an effort by several authors to bridge the gap between SDL theory and practice. It was one of the first publications to highlight some specific case studies as examples of how SDL principles and research findings can be translated into actual practice in an organization, profession, or community. It provides some new understanding of how self-directed, individualized learning can be and is being promoted. For the interested reader Knowles and Associates (1984), in another excellent source, describe several examples of andragogical and SDL principles being applied in a variety of organizations and institutions.

In essence both research and practice have shown that autonomous learning works! Adult learning does not need to take place in the presence of a teacher nor in a traditional setting where a didactic presentation of information is the primary delivery mode. This should be good news for the busy human resources manager or training specialist who frequently must respond to learning requirements within the organization that outstrip available financial and teaching resources.

As several authors demonstrated, giving some of the responsibility for learning back to learners is not only possible, but in many cases it is more beneficial than other approaches. For example, employees with complex and busy schedules can learn some needed skills or information at their convenience through self-study, self-directed learning modules, and even study at home. Some technical and professional staff whose increased productivity depends on continuous learning because of the rapidity of change can benefit by being able to access information through a resource center. Some organizations even have been successful in providing basic orientation information through SDL modes.

What Can Be Done?

Brookfield's *Sourcebook* contains a wealth of examples and suggestions pertaining to what can be done in applying knowledge about self-directed learning. This section will highlight several of these.

1. Think about the type of learning that might benefit a particular trainee or that might be the most appropriate for attaining certain skills or knowledge. There are at least three ways of categorizing learning that can be considered: instrumental, dialogic, and self-reflective.
2. The transformation of our perspectives and understandings about life is crucial as we acquire and apply new knowledge to our work. Trainers can provide opportunities for self-directed learners to move consistently toward more authentic meaning perspectives through dialogue by promoting self-reflection and self-knowledge and by helping them understand a variety of alternatives.
3. Learners can diagnose many of their own learning needs, but training specialists or human resource managers may need to facilitate such diagnostic efforts through the development of instruments or by providing opportunities for trainers to discuss their needs with others.
4. Learners are capable of planning much of their own learning once they have some understanding of individual needs. Learning contracts are one of the tools that has been used successfully for such planning.
5. Several self-directed, individualized instructional strategies are available. These include such activities as planning various learning options, acquiring a variety of learning resources, negotiating individual learning plans with students, helping learners

develop self-confidence, and promoting critical thinking and evaluation skills.

6. Self-directed learners frequently require knowledge about various learning options and resources. Thus, there will be a need to locate and acquire a variety of learning materials, often placing them in the organization's learning resource center.

7. Self-directed learning does not always need to take place individually. Study groups, working with a mentor, and dialoguing with others electronically are some of the techniques that have been employed successfully in various organizations.

There are ways that self-directed learning principles have been used outside those described in this sourcebook. Each organization or institution interested in exploring possibilities to meet its own training or educational needs should examine the type of knowledge required of employees or students, determine available educational resources, and consider what can be done with SDL to meet some of the organizational needs.

Some Potential Concerns and Challenges

Meeting many organizational education or training needs through self-directed learning and individualized instructional approaches is possible in terms of what is already known through research and practice. However, there are several potential concerns and challenges that will need to be considered. This section describes some of them.

1. Promoting critical thinking, reflection, and analysis is possible, but it will be a challenge with some learners. Many educators of adults will require special training or knowledge of certain techniques that promote critical thinking.

2. Initially, extra resources may need to be expended as SDL principles are incorporated into an organization's educational or training programs. A workable learning resource center will require space, computers, software, and other instructional resources. Instructional staff may need to be retrained. However, over time the organization's instructional costs may diminish as more people become self-directed in their learning efforts.

3. There may be some initial hesitancy, frustration, or confusion among learners as an organization incorporates SDL principles. Sensitive, trained facilitators will be required to help such people overcome initial problems.

4. Self-directed learning capability will vary from learner to learner. Trainers and educators of adults may need to provide extra initial support for dependent learners as they build individualized learning skills and confidence.

5. Evaluating self-directed or individualized learning often can be difficult. Creative ways for assessing learner progress may need to be found.

6. One of the techniques that can be used to promote SDL is matching individual learners with preceptors or mentors who will guide some of the educational activities. However, finding and training such support personnel can be difficult.

7. In many organizations there will be some institutional and program constraints to overcome. Traditional expectations, rules, regulations, resistance to change, and mandated requirements are some of these. Human resource managers will need to obtain cooperation from top management as well as trainers to meet such challenges.

Future Needs

Applying some of what we know about SDL and overcoming various concerns and challenges will require a commitment by an organization or institution to move forward. Such a commitment, at face value, may not seem worth it. "If it ain't broke, don't fix it!" as the saying goes. However, one of the messages spoken loud and clear in the *Sourcebook* is that it is worth it for many reasons. Learners can be successful and, in many instances, ultimately appear to achieve at levels greater than in approaches that are more teacher- or institutionally-directed. For many with busy and complex lives, attaining needed knowledge often is possible only via self-directed modes. There is even some evidence that organizations can save money while still meeting training needs through individualized learning techniques.

But, what are some of the future needs that should be considered as an agency contemplates incorporating SDL approaches into its training and educational efforts? This final section describes four such needs.

1. Some existing organizational policies will inhibit self-directed learning at either the learner, educator, or institutional level. There is a need to examine those policies that have an impact on training or education and change them if necessary or create new ones.

2. There are several ethical questions that will need to be raised and addressed in many organizations. These pertain to such issues as maintaining quality in learning outcomes, the exact roles facilitators should play in self-directed learning pursuits, and the actual content areas that can be studied when learners are given more responsibility for decision making.

3. One of the concerns expressed by most authors associated with the *Sourcebook* pertains to assisting learners in obtaining critical analysis or thinking skills. Organizational leaders will need to find ways of helping learners form good questions, obtain information-seeking skills, and carry out self-evaluation.

4. It appears as though increasingly more computer-supported resources and electronic communication techniques will be available for self-directed learners. Organizations will need to find ways of accommodating and incorporating such innovations.

The New Directions for Continuing Education Sourcebook Number 25 provides a wealth of information pertaining to how SDL principles can be used for educational or training efforts. Understanding some of the contributions the publication made in advancing knowledge about self-directed, individualized learning in conjunction with the other publications reviewed in this book, should be beneficial as organizations and educators of adults consider ways of incorporating such principles into their own educational efforts.

References

Ash, C. R. (1985). Applying principles of self-directed learning in the health professions. In S. D. Brookfield (Ed.), *Self-directed learning: From theory to practice* (New Directions for Continuing Education, Number 25, 63-74). San Francisco, CA: Jossey-Bass.

Bauer, B. A. (1985). Self-directed learning in a graduate adult education program. In S. D. Brookfield (Ed.), *Self-directed learning: From theory to practice* (New Directions for Continuing Education, Number 25, 41-50). San Francisco, CA: Jossey-Bass.

Brockett, R. G. (1985). A response to Brookfield's critical paradigm of self-directed adult learning. *Adult Education Quarterly, 36,* 55-59.

Brockett, R. G., & Hiemstra, R. (1985). Bridging the theory-practice gap in self-directed learning. In S. D. Brookfield (Ed.), *Self-directed learning: From theory to practice* (New Directions for Continuing Education, Number 25, 31-40). San Francisco, CA: Jossey-Bass.

Brockett, R. G., & Hiemstra, R. (1991). *Self-direction in adult learning: Perspectives on theory, research, and practice.* London, UK: Routledge.

Brookfield, S. D. (1978). Individualising adult learning: An English experiment. *Lifelong Learning: The Adult Years, 1*(7), 18-20.

Brookfield, S. D. (1980). *Independent adult learning.* Unpublished doctoral dissertation, University of Leicester (England).

Brookfield, S. D. (1981a). The adult learning iceberg: A critical review of the work of Allen Tough. *Adult Education* (UK), *54,* 110-118.

Brookfield, S. D. (1981b). Independent adult learning. *Studies in Adult Education, 13,* 15-27.

Brookfield, S. D. (1982). Successful independent learning of adults of low educational attainment in Britain: A parallel educational universe. *Proceedings of the 23rd Annual Adult Education Research Conference,* 48-53. Lincoln, NE: University of Nebraska-Lincoln, Department of Adult and Continuing Education.

Brookfield, S. D. (1984a). *Adult learners, adult education and the community.* New York, NY: Teachers College Press.

Brookfield, S. D. (1984b). Self-directed learning: A critical paradigm. *Adult Education Quarterly, 35,* 59-71.

Brookfield, S. D. (1985a). Analyzing a critical paradigm of self-directed learning: A response. *Adult Education Quarterly, 36,* 60-64.

Brookfield, S. D. (1985b). Sources in self-directed learning theory and practice. In S. D. Brookfield (Ed.), *Self-directed learning: From theory to practice* (New Directions for Continuing Education, Number 25, 87-90). San Francisco, CA: Jossey-Bass.

Brookfield, S. D. (1985c). The continuing educator and self-directed learning in the community. In S. D. Brookfield (Ed.), *Self-directed learning: From theory to practice* (New Directions for Continuing Education, Number 25, 75-85). San Francisco, CA: Jossey-Bass.

Brookfield, S. D. (1985d). Self-directed learning: A critical review of research. In S. D. Brookfield (Ed.), *Self-directed learning: From theory to practice* (New Directions for Continuing Education, Number 25, 5-16). San Francisco, CA: Jossey-Bass.

Brookfield, S. D. (1989). *Developing critical thinkers: Challenging adults to explore alternative ways of thinking and acting.* San Francisco, CA: Jossey-Bass.

Carr, D. (1985). Self-directed learning in cultural institutions. In S. D. Brookfield (Ed.), *Self-directed learning: From theory to practice* (New Directions for Continuing Education, Number 25, 51-62). San Francisco, CA: Jossey-Bass.

Hiemstra, R., & Sisco, B. (1990). *Individualizing instruction: Making learning personal, empowering, and successful.* San Francisco, CA: Jossey-Bass.

Houle, C. O. (1961). *The inquiring mind.* Madison, WI: The University of Wisconsin Press.

Knowles, M. S. (1970). *The modern practice of adult education.* NY: Association Press.

Knowles, M. S. & Associates. (1984). *Andragogy in action: Applying modern principles of adult learning.* San Francisco, CA: Jossey-Bass.

Mezirow, J. (1975). *Education for perspective transformation: Women's re-entry programs in community colleges.* NY: Center for Adult Development, Teachers College, Columbia University.

Mezirow, J. (1978). Perspective transformation. *Adult Education, 28,* 100-10.

Mezirow, J. (1981). A critical theory of adult learning and education. *Adult Education, 32,* 3-24.

Mezirow, J. (1985). A critical theory of self-directed learning. In S. D. Brookfield (Ed.), *Self-directed learning: From theory to practice* (New Directions for Continuing Education, Number 25, 17-30). San Francisco, CA: Jossey-Bass.

Mezirow, J. (1991). *Transformative dimensions of adult learning.* San Francisco, CA: Jossey-Bass.

Mezirow, J. & Associates. (1991). *Fostering critical reflection in adulthood: A guide to transformative and emancipatory learning.* San Francisco, CA: Jossey-Bass.

Tough, A. M. (1966). The assistance obtained by adult self-teachers. *Adult Education, 17,* 30-37.

Tough, A. M. (1967). *Learning without a teacher: A study of tasks and assistance during adult self-teaching projects.* Toronto, Ontario: Ontario Institute for Studies in Education.

Tough, A. M. (1971). *The adult's learning projects.* Toronto, Ontario: Ontario Institute for Studies in Education.

Tough, A. M. (1979). *The adult's learning projects,* (2nd ed.). Austin, TX: Learning Concepts.

Chapter Eleven

Understanding and Facilitating Adult Learning

Lucy M. Guglielmino on Stephen Brookfield

Dr. Guglielmino is Professor of Adult Education and Chairperson of the Department of Educational Leadership at Florida Atlantic University. She developed the Self-Directed Learning Readiness Scale (SDLRS), *which is the most frequently used instrument for measuring readiness for self-directed learning.*

The centrality of the concept of self-direction in learning is established early in Stephen Brookfield's book, *Understanding and Facilitating Adult Learning.* While recognizing the allure and insistent pressures of the institutional and societal context that promotes traditional instruction, Brookfield stands firm in the need to promote empowerment and self-direction in learners. Noting that the vast majority of studies of participation in adult learning focus on enrollees in formal courses, he asserts ". . . it is both naive and arrogant to assume that adult learning is restricted to [such] settings" (p. 4), acknowledging the importance and frequency of adult learning outside of traditional classroom settings. He then presents six principles of effective practice in facilitating adult learning. The last of these identifies the aim of facilitation as the "nurturing of self-directed, empowered adults" (p. 11). The classroom setting, then, becomes simply one of the learning resources for a self-directed adult learner rather than the primary mode of learning it is often perceived to be. The expert facilitator, rather than dispensing knowledge and ensuring that all the participants can replicate it on a test, accepts the responsibility of responding to and developing "proactive, initiating individuals engaged in a continuous re-creation of their personal relationships, work worlds, and social circumstances . . ." (p. 11).

While references to self-directed learning are frequent throughout the book, self-direction in learning is the specific topic of the third and fourth chapters and a section of Chapter Seven. These passages are a refreshing mixture of philosophy and pragmatism and are as valuable for the questions they raise as for the information they provide. In fact, one of the major contributions of this work to the body of literature on self-direction in learning arises from Brookfield practicing what he preaches. He emphasizes the importance of critical reflection in self-directed learners; and, logically, devotes a significant portion of his discussion of self-direction to his own critical reflections on the topic.

Definition and Conceptualization of Self-Direction in Learning

In Chapter Three Brookfield addresses the definition of self-direction in learning and explores the concept, raising several important issues. The first relates to definition. He points out that the most commonly used definitions of self-directedness, such as Knowles' (1975) and Tough's (1966, 1967) focus on "externally observable learning activities or behaviors," (p. 40) such as assessing needs and planning, implementing, and evaluating learning experiences.

He advocates exploration of the concept of self-direction in learning in terms of mental dispositions but points out that some common assumptions in this area of study may not be accurate. He discusses Witkin's (1949, 1950) field dependence/field independence research and points out the connection made by Holtzman (1982) between field independent styles of learning and mature adulthood. He also mentions Pratt's (1984) comment that field independent styles and successful self-directed learning traditionally are closely linked, then interjects a concern. Describing field independence as "the single-minded pursuit of specified learning goals" (p. 42), he points out that the critical reflection that he sees as an important part of self-direction in learning involves some aspects more commonly connected with field dependence: "awareness of the contextuality and contingency of knowledge and . . . appreciation of the culturally constructed nature of value frameworks, social codes, and belief systems." He thus rejects the claim to field independence as a parallel to self-directedness in learning.

Based on his own (Brookfield, 1980, 1981), Thiel's (1984), and Danis and Tremblay's (1985) research, Brookfield emphasizes what becomes an important theme in this work: the value of learning networks made up of individuals pursuing similar interests and the extent to which interaction within this type of network is characteristic of successful self-directed learners. These findings would tend to indicate a relationship between some of the characteristics of field *dependent* learners and readiness for self-direction. Because of the current emphasis in human resource development on self-managing work teams, these findings and further research in this area should be of particular interest to facilitators of adult learning in business and industry.

Brookfield's definition of self-directed learning fully emerges near the end of Chapter Three:

> Self-directed learning as the mode of learning characteristic of an adult who is in the process of realizing his or her adulthood is concerned as much with an internal change of consciousness as with the external management of instructional events . . . The most complete form of self-directed learning occurs when process and reflection are married in the adult's pursuit of meaning.

Research on Self-Direction in Learning

Three other questions raised by Brookfield in Chapter Three relate to the body of research on self-directed learning. First, pointing out that the preponderance of subjects studied in research on self-directed learning have been educationally advantaged, middle class Americans, he challenges the validity of the " . . . conventional wisdom that adults . . . (as a generic category) are self-directed learners . . ." (p. 52). While he applauds self-directedness as a prescriptive aim, he asserts that it cannot be assumed as an empirical descriptor.

Brookfield also addresses the issue of research approaches, contending that the predominance of the use of Tough's (1967, 1968, 1979, 1982) interview schedules and prompt sheets (or modifications thereof) and Guglielmino's (1977) *Self-Directed Learning Readiness Scale* (SDLRS) have had some impacts that require examination. He points out that because such measures are available, the design of research in self-direction in learning may be shaped by their very availability. Further, in the case of interviews based on Tough's methodology, the learning projects that are reported by participants may be influenced by the examples given in discussions preceding the actual questioning of the interviewee.

He also points out that some adults might be intimidated by or suspicious of such "investigative hardware" as formalized interviews or instruments, referring primarily to working class adults, ethnic minorities, and recently arrived immigrants (p. 52). His 1986 conclusion that the SDLRS is useful only for adults with average or above-average levels of education might be tempered by the availability of a new form (Guglielmino, 1989) that was developed specifically for adults of low educational attainment and non-native English speakers, which appeared after the publication of his book. However, Brookfield clearly prefers an open-ended, conversational style of interviewing as a means of gathering information about self-directed learners. Brookfield's third concern in this area is the lack of research emphasis on the quality of learning achieved through self-directed study, an omission that he feels it is essential to address.

Facilitating Self-Directed Learning

In Chapter Four Brookfield discusses some of the differences between facilitation of self-directed learning in the individual mode and in the group mode. Importantly, he clarifies the point that the aim of facilitation is the same regardless of whether the individual or group mode is used. That aim is to assist adults to become "self-directed, critically aware individuals capable of imagining and then realizing alternative ways of thinking and living" (p. 68).

Brookfield also asserts that neither mode is superior to the other. He points out the value of one-to-one interaction between learner and facilitator in assisting learners to "become more aware of their unique learning styles and to develop a sense of direct control over the method and direction of learning" (p. 61). He also emphasizes the value of several aspects of the group process as motivators for further learning by the self-directed learner. Validation of one's own experiences and ideas, the acquisition of new insights and interpretations based on interchanges with fellow learners, and the enthusiasm generated by this process are among the most potent benefits mentioned. His discussion early in this chapter could serve as a valuable antidote to the persistent myth that self-directed learning can only refer to an individual working alone. He emphasizes the value of group interaction and feedback to the self-directed learner and states that a mix of individual and group modes is "generally the most effective process for enhancing adult learning."

For the individual who has been trained as a didactic instructor (or who has been thrust into a teacher/trainer mode and has simply modeled his or her past experiences in group learning), Brookfield's section on the role of facilitators will be especially helpful. He summarizes some of the characteristics of facilitators and the facilitative relationship, citing extensively from adult education literature. In this summation he asserts the importance of helping learners to become aware of their own learning styles and processes and thus devotes a great deal of attention to Smith's (1982a, 1982b, 1983) work on the process of learning how to learn.

Considerations for Facilitators

Brookfield points out two important cautions to the individual who has become committed to the facilitation of self-directed learning. First, he emphasizes that adults will not all be equally prepared to engage in self-directed learning. Some learners will embrace the concept enthusiastically, but others will not initially respond positively to being expected to accept a greater responsibility for their own learning. While adult education literature tends to expound on the value and benefits of self-direction in learning, it is vital to remember that most adults are products of an educational system in which a didactic approach to instruction predominates. In essence, these individuals have been trained to be *dependent, teacher-directed* learners in a classroom context. Some of them will feel liberated and energized by self-directed approaches; others may be intimidated by expectations that they will assume a greater role in the design of their own learning. Some will be resentful, feeling that the teacher is not doing his or her job. Levels of experience with individual learning projects or group-facilitated, self-directed learning will also vary. All of these factors combine to produce differential levels of readiness for self-directed learning, which will require varying levels of assistance from learning facilitators.

Secondly, Brookfield describes the difficulties inherent in attempting to realize fully the facilitation of self-directed learning in an institutional context. Grading policies, state or institutionally mandated curricular requirements, and adherence of administrators and other faculty to traditional concepts of didactic instruction may preclude total self-direction. He goes on to report in detail on a number of "experiments in self-directed learning" in institutional contexts (pp. 69-81) and then extracts from these attempts five central themes. The first major theme identified is the centrality of learning contracts as a means of planning for self-directed learning in institutional contexts. Although the training context is not mentioned by Brookfield in this section, it is interesting to note that in some of the companies where self-directed learning is being employed, learning contracts have become commonly used. Based on performance evaluations and employee development goals, the learning contracts can become an integral part of the annual goal-setting process (Guglielmino & Guglielmino, 1988). Other themes noted include:

1. The necessity for preparation of both learning facilitators and learners for self-directed learning formats.
2. The value of peer learning groups as resources for self-directed learners and the advisability of facilitators encouraging their early development.
3. The alteration of traditional time commitments required by self-directed learning formats.
4. The perceived benefits of facilitating self-direction in learning.

Brookfield concludes that despite the initial frustration, ambiguity, and resentment felt by some learners when they are initially invited to take greater responsibility for their own learning, the approach ultimately wins the approval of the majority of learners and facilitators. Learners, in particular, often refer to the liberating and motivating impact of self-directed learning.

Incorporation of Aspects of Self-Directed Learning into Formal Settings

In Chapter Seven, which focuses on learning in formal settings, Brookfield points out that the literature on adult education has not reflected a great deal of concern with training in business and industry, with the notable exceptions of Kidd (1969), Knowles (1984), and Nadler (1984), among others. He delineates some differences between adult education in the business community and in other settings that may explain this lack. The major difference relates to purpose and, therefore, to evaluative criteria. While personal growth and development are the major emphases of most adult education outside of business and industry, that focus becomes secondary to organizational profitability within the business world.

Brookfield urges increased recognition by college and university educators of educational efforts within business and industry. He summarizes some of the data and reports that illuminate the reality that private industry is a major provider of education for adults in terms of numbers served, programs offered, and dollars expended. He further notes the increasing interest of HRD professionals in doctoral programs in adult education. Emphasizing the need for incorporating collaborative and critically reflective elements into business and industry training programs, he notes Peters and Waterman's mention of these characteristics in their study of America's most successful companies (1982). He then suggests, as a possible role for educators in the training process, the introduction of efforts to help participants become more aware of their own potential for self-development. He cites from the literature a number of authors and programs that approach or partially reflect his guidelines for effective facilitation. Especially helpful is his inclusion of an international perspective.

Since this book was written, there has been a greater recognition by business and industry, especially within the United States, that great benefits can result from the promotion and support of self-directed learning efforts among their employees. Research conducted within major organizations has established a link between levels of readiness for self-directed learning and employee performance (Guglielmino & Guglielmino, 1988; Roberts, 1986). Self-directed work teams have been found to be extremely productive and enable the reduction of managerial positions (Wellins, Byham, & Wilson, 1991). Materials have been developed to enhance individual and organizational readiness for a managerial paradigm in which employees assume a major role (Glaser, 1991; Guglielmino & Guglielmino, 1991; Harper & Harper, 1989).22

Conclusion

The major contribution of Brookfield's *Understanding and Facilitating Adult Learning* to the literature on self-directed learning is, as previously stated, the application of critical reflection, which leads to a closer examination of definitions, research methodology, and every aspect of what we think we know about self-direction in learning. Regardless of whether one agrees with all of Brookfield's answers, it is important to consider the questions. Two other recurrent themes throughout the sections dealing with self-directed learning seem particularly noteworthy. Brookfield emphasizes the value of networks of fellow learners as resources and support groups for self-directed learners. This is an area that has not been thoroughly researched and merits further examination. The second theme that permeates these sections is Brookfield's concept of the facilitator's responsibility for encouraging critical reflection and presenting alternative viewpoints, as well as aiding participants in understanding their learning styles, developing learning plans, and identifying possible resources or learning approaches.

Other valuable aspects include the thoughtful comments on some of the contradictions inherent in promoting self-directed learning within the usual education and training environments, coupled with an examination of actual situations where such efforts have been made. The references to both philosophy and practice and the discussion of espoused theories and theories of use are valuable for the practitioner who wants to implement new approaches. Presentations of possibilities and benefits are accompanied by a discussion of potential roadblocks and negative reactions, leaving the reader prepared for a broad spectrum of responses to implementation efforts.

References

Brookfield, S. D. (1980). *Independent adult learning.* Unpublished doctoral dissertation, Department of Adult Education, University of Leicester.

Brookfield, S. D. (1981). Independent adult learning. *Studies in Adult Education, 13*(1), 15-27.

Brookfield, S. D. (1986). *Understanding and facilitating adult learning.* San Francisco, CA: Jossey-Bass.

Danis, C. & Tremblay, N. (1985). Critical analysis of adult learning principles from a self-directed learner's perspective. *Proceedings of the Adult Education Research Conference,* No. 26. Tempe, AZ: Arizona State University.

Glaser, R. (1991). *How independent is our team?* King of Prussia, PA: Organization Design and Development.

Guglielmino, L. M. (1977). Development of the self-directed learning readiness scale. (Doctoral dissertation, The University of Georgia.) *Dissertation Abstracts International, 38,* 6467A.

Guglielmino, L. M. (1989). Development of an adult basic education form of the self-directed learning readiness scale. In H. B. Long and Associates, *Self-directed learning: Emerging theory and practice.* Norman, OK: Oklahoma Research Center for Continuing Professional and Higher Education.

Guglielmino, L. M., & Guglielmino, P. J. (1988). Self-directed learning in business and industry: An information age imperative. In H. B. Long and Associates, *Self-directed learning: Application and theory.* Lifelong Learning Research/Publication Project, Department of Adult Education, University of Georgia.

Guglielmino, L. M., & Guglielmino, P. J. (1991). *Expanding your readiness for self-directed learning.* King of Prussia, PA: Organization Design and Development.

Harper, R., & Harper, A. (1989). *Succeeding as a self-directed work team.* Croton-on-Hudson, NY: MW Corporation.

Holtzman, W. H. (1982). Cross cultural comparisons of personality development in Mexico and the United States. In D. A. Wagner and H. W. Stevenson (Eds.), *Cultural perspectives on child development.* NY: W. H. Freeman.

Kidd, J. R. (1969). *Education for perspective.* Toronto, Ontario: Peter Martin.

Knowles, M. S. (1975). *Self-directed learning: A guide for learners and teachers.* NY: Cambridge Books.

Knowles, M. S. and Associates. (1984). *Andragogy in action: Applying modern principles of adult learning.* San Francisco, CA: Jossey-Bass.

Nadler, L. (Ed.) (1984). *The handbook of human resource development.* NY: Wiley.

Peters, T. J., & Waterman, R. H. (1982). *In search of excellence: Lessons from America's best run companies.* NY: Harper & Row.

Pratt, D. D. (1984). Andragogical assumptions: Some counter-intuitive logic. *Proceedings of the Adult Education Research Conference,* No. 25. Raleigh, NC: North Carolina State University.

Roberts, D. G. (1986). A study of the use of the self-directed learning readiness scale as related to selected organization variables. (Doctoral dissertation, The George Washington University.) *Dissertation Abstracts International,* 47, 1218A.

Smith, R. M. (1982a). *Learning how to learn: Applied learning theory for adults.* New York, NY: Cambridge Books.

Smith, R. M. (1982b). Some programmatic and instructional implications of the learning how to learn concept. *Proceedings of the Adult Education Research Conference,* No. 23. Lincoln, NE: University of Nebraska.

Smith, R. M. (1983). Helping adults learn how to learn. *New directions for continuing education,* No. 19. San Francisco, CA: Jossey-Bass.

Thiel, J. P. (1984). Successful self-directed learner's learning styles. *Proceedings of the Adult Education Research Conference,* No. 25. Raleigh, NC: North Carolina State University.

Tough, A. M. (1966). The assistance obtained by adult self-teachers. *Adult Education* (USA.), *17* (1), 30-37.

Tough, A. M. (1967). Learning without a teacher: A study of tasks and assistance during adult self-teaching projects. *Education Research Series,* No. 3. Toronto, Ontario: Ontario Institute for Studies in Education.

Tough, A. M. (1968). *Why adults learn: A study of the major reasons for beginning and continuing a learning project.* Toronto, Ontario: Ontario Institute for Studies in Education.

Tough, A. M. (1979). *The adult's learning projects: A fresh approach to theory and practice in adult learning.* Toronto, Ontario: Ontario Institute for Studies in Education.

Tough, A. M. (1982). *Intentional changes: A fresh approach to helping people change.* New York, NY: Cambridge Books.

Wellins, R. S., Byham, W. C., & Wilson, J. M. (1991). *Empowered teams.* San Francisco, CA: Jossey-Bass.

Witkin, H. A. (1949). The nature and importance of individual differences in perception. *Journal of Personality, 18,* 145-70.

Witkin, H. A. (1950). Individual differences in ease of perception of embedded figures. *Journal of Personality, 19,* 1-15.

Chapter Twelve

Self-Directed Adult Learning:
A Critical Paradigm Revisited

George E. Spear on Rosemary Caffarella and Judith O'Donnell

*Dr. Spear is Professor Emeritus of Education at The University of Missouri —
Kansas City. He is a former editor of The American Association for Adult and
Continuing Education's* Lifelong Learning. *Dr. Spear was co-founder of the
Master of Arts in Education Program at UMKC and of the National Center for
Resource Development in Adult Education. His major research and writing
interests in recent years have been associated with adult self-directed learning.*

Reviews of literature at their best are not merely collections and
summaries of a period and a field of study but become themselves
major contributions to that body of literature. They add dimension
and insight beyond the limits of individual studies and may direct
attention to both the shortcomings and the potential found within the
area in question.

Such is the case with Caffarella's and O'Donnell's article, "Self-
Directed Adult Learning: A Critical Paradigm Revisited," which
appeared in the *Adult Education Quarterly, 37* (4), 1987.* This review
capped a series of summaries of self-directed learning that began
when Coolican (1974) identified seven studies, including her own dissertation, that had used the approach initiated by Allen Tough (1978).
Tough's seminal work, *The Adult's Learning Projects,* clearly established self-directed learning as a major adult learning mode and
loosed a stream of interest that was to become a flood of popular
research productivity.

---

*Several evolutions and refinements of this paper appeared between 1985 and 1987,
but the Delphi panel considers this to be the basic, standard version of the work.

By 1987, Caffarella and O'Donnell could draw on a substantial body of research and conceptual literature that had begun to chart new directions and turn up new discoveries. They acknowledged the preceding reviews of Brookfield (1984), Mocker and Spear (1982), and Tough (1978) as providing a foundation for the building of their work. However, with benefit of the accumulated knowledge, plus their own insight and analytic expertise, the article here proved to be the hallmark review of the two decades following Tough's original study and publication. Tough (1978) reviewed the research spawned by his earlier efforts and identified 24 studies that replicated his own. That number had increased to 50 in the next four years (Tough, 1982). His review found remarkable consistency in the findings of the various studies regarding the average number of projects adults conducted in a year, the hours spent in learning, and the utilization of resources. However, he also concluded that there had been little added by the replications to the concept, theory, and research methodology that he had originally put in place.

Mocker and Spear (1982) sought a definition of self-directed learning that would set it apart from formal and other less traditional types of education. Basing their work on a model of control of goals and means of learning, they found considerable research that purported to be about self-directed learning that was, in fact, dealing with other entirely different types of learning and educational formats. They noted also that researchers had begun to break away from simply replicating Tough's work and suggested that recognition of environmental forces influencing self-directed learning was an emerging trend in the new research.

Brookfield (1984) turned a critical eye on the research in the field, first joining Boshier (1983) in seeking to attach school words such as *teaching* and *education* to the concept and to disconnect the word *learning*. (It may be noted that the term *self-directed learning* has withstood various assaults and seems now to be the term of choice of most writers and researchers in the field.) Brookfield then took aim at four major flaws he found in the research to date:

1. Subpopulations from outside the white middle class were substantially under-represented in the populations studied.
2. The research that had been conducted was essentially quantitative in nature, and there was not a reasonable balance of qualitative research to enhance our understanding of the phenomenon.
3. There was an emphasis on individual behavior almost to the exclusion of social context.
4. The research failed to deal with issues of social and political change.

With these reviews as launching points, the authors conducted additional reviews of original sources and identified 29 references that had not been cited in any of the previous reviews. From this pool of discovery and knowledge, they concluded that the various studies could be divided into five distinct categories. Those categories were:

1. Verification studies after Tough.
2. Nature of the method of self-directed learning.
3. Nature of the individual learner.
4. Nature of the philosophical position.
5. Policy questions.

Not surprisingly, the major area of concentration was with verification studies, next in methodology studies, and an evident growing interest in the nature of the individual learner.

For purposes of this chapter, the same section headings will be used as appeared in the original article by Caffarella and O'Donnell. Also, I will add comments that did not appear in the original work and these will be clearly identified.

Verification Studies

Caffarella and O'Donnell cited a number of verification studies that had confirmed the expected presence of self-directed learning and then agreed with Brookfield (1984) that for the most part the populations were middle class. However, they noted that Brockett (1985) had identified several studies dealing with non-middle class populations and that had not been taken into account by Brookfield in his criticisms. They also found that descriptions of populations were often sketchy at best and that Tough's question and probe interview technique should be supplemented by other approaches to test for interviewer contamination.

In the end, however, Caffarella and O'Donnell called for an end to the monotonous parade of verifications with American and British populations and suggested that some less predictable outcomes might accrue from research among minority, hard-to-reach, and foreign culture groups.

Comment

Verification studies of Tough's work have presented graduate students an almost irresistible opportunity for producing dissertations that were highly topical and easy to research and write, with fairly predictable outcomes that did not beg explanation. Although such studies eventually proved to be overkill, they firmly established self-directed learning as perhaps the chief means by which adults gain knowledge and skills. They proved that such learning was pervasive and cleared the way for successor research to get on with better understanding the phenomenon.

Nature of the Method

Research questions in this category are directed toward the process by which adults engage in and pursue learning. Caffarella and O'Donnell divided this category into four subcategories:

1. The planning process and conceptualization of planning.
2. Types of planners.
3. Types of learning resources used.
4. Competencies related to method.

The Planning Process

Tough (1971) originally focused on the various planners of adult learning projects, and Caffarella and O'Donnell note that both Tough and Knowles (1975) presented, with some detail, the specific steps taken by adults in planning self-directed learning. Both processes suggested the learners began with a clear idea of what needed to be done in order to achieve their goals and that they then made all the necessary provisions.

The authors note, however, that Spear and Mocker (1984) offered a different perspective derived from open-ended interviews with adults with less than high school completion. These learners, rather than engaging in detailed preplanning, built learning projects from whatever resources their environments happened to provide. They called this determining effect of the environment the *organizing circumstance* (see Chapter 9 of this book).

Research needs cited by Caffarella and O'Donnell were for more understanding of how adults choose, plan, and engage in self-directed learning projects. Also, they said more needs to be known about the effects of environment and educational level, the skills needed to find and use learning opportunities and resources, and how learners perceive the organizing of their projects.

Comments

It would seem likely that the planning steps detected by both Tough and Knowles were influenced by deeply seated familiarity with the process of planning in formal education. It might have been simple to ascribe to self-directed learning the same process of decisions and actions.

The organizing circumstance, however, identified existing resources in the environment including experts, models, books in family libraries, and television specials. The availability of these resources had the effect of structuring the learning plan or process while at the same time limiting its scope. The adult learned as best he or she could from whatever opportunities and resources were at hand.

Types of Planners

Tough's original study (1971) and Penland in his national study (1979) are the two major efforts identifying types of planners used in constructing self-directed learning projects. Tough found that the planning function was performed by the individual, resource materials, an expert or helper, and by planning groups. Penland saw more emphasis on planning by self, directive materials, and expert helpers. There was less reliance on group planning activity.

Although both studies called for more information on planner types, subsequent research has demonstrated little interest in that element of self-directed learning.

Comment

If indeed the learner himself/herself is the major project planner, it would follow that the process rather than the type of planner is of greatest interest and significance.

Types of Learning Resources

While types of planners seems to have generated little curiosity, researchers have pursued with some vigor the types of resources adults use in their self-directed projects. The authors cited nearly a dozen studies that suggested diversity among various populations. The list included learning cliques, friends and acquaintances, radio, university field days, informal discussions with peers, books, pamphlets, and special interest groups. Libraries and librarians, they note, were not major resources.

The issue of identifying and accessing necessary resources has been seen as a problem and challenge to adult educators for a decade or more (Brookfield, 1981; Houle, 1984; Penland, 1979; Tough, 1978). Nearly all forms of communication are resources, but such generic lists are not particularly informative.

Comment

Some businesses and similar organizations have begun to provide resources for employees in an attempt to improve productivity and assist in problem solving. They have collected documents, audio and video materials, and lists of in-house experts that might pertain to some of the functions in the organization. Some organizations have even staffed separate, on-site learning centers to assist employees with job-associated problems and demands. However, there is still little information in self-directed learning literature that can guide those who would establish such resource facilities.

Competencies Related to the Method

What does the learner need to be able to do to carry out a self-directed learning project? It is obvious that certain skills are necessary and that some people are likely to have those skills to a greater degree than do others.

Caffarella and O'Donnell turn to Knowles (1975) and Tough (1971) for suggestions. They cite Knowles' suggestions for an "ability to relate to peers collaboratively; to diagnose their own needs; to translate needs to objectives; to identify resources; and to evaluate."

Tough focuses on the ability to know what help was needed, select resources, secure help, analyze, plan the entire project, and evaluate.

Caffarella and Caffarella (1986) tested the Knowles-Tough listing using learning contracts with graduate students and found positive effects on three of twelve competencies. Kasworm (1983) found less specifically that learning contracts were a benefit in increasing awareness and skill in self-directed learning.

Comment

The competencies needed for effective self-directed learning may be arrived at in part by common sense, but they require additional exploration and verification through research. At the same time, those competencies seem teachable in the way study skills are taught in traditional schools. However, simply forcing students into self-directed studies in a traditional, authority-centered classroom may not be the most effective approach to teaching such skills.

Nature of the Individual

In the literature on the nature of the individual learner, the authors found five sub-categories separating areas of focus. Those were:

1. Demographic data.
2. Learning or cognitive style.
3. Readiness.
4. Locus of control.
5. Personality characteristics.

The amount of research generated within each subcategory has proven generally inconclusive, if not conflicting. To date, the greatest interest has centered on readiness, largely because of the quantifiable *Self-Directed Learning Readiness Scale* (SDLRS) constructed by Guglielmino (1977).

Correlation studies are both easy and relatively safe, so use of the SDLRS has been fairly popular. High readiness scores have been correlated with originality of thinking, ability to produce analogies, creative experiences and achievement, and right brain learning styles and thinking (Torrance & Mourad, 1978). Also, relationships have been found with quantity of self-directed projects, learner satisfaction, and self-concept.

The SDLRS has drawn some criticism from both Brookfield (1984) and Brockett (1985). Both found the scale oriented toward school-like skills and thus biased toward some populations. Brockett, however, encouraged its use with certain qualified groups and populations.

Also noted was a new perspective identified with Oddi (1984, 1986) in which readiness for self-directed learning is viewed as an attribute of personality rather than an instructional process. Assuming a subjectivity of personality as opposed to an objective intellectual process, the Oddi theory suggests *a priori* conditions as foundations for readiness.

Comment

The search for personality traits, as well as verification of skills and attitudes, continues to command attention. There have been no major breakthroughs since Caffarella and O'Donnell presented this article. The research needs they set forth were for quantifiable, experimental designs with randomly selected subjects. Also, they called for greater in-depth, qualitative research to provide increased clarity to what is at best a sketchy picture of the able adult self-directed learner.

Nature of the Philosophical Position

The authors begin this section with the disclaimer that no research supports the points presented. Instead, conceptual articles have set forth philosophical positions as matters affecting perspectives regarding self-directed learning. They cite Mezirow (1985) and Brookfield (1985) both seeking to restrict the definition of learning to that of mental activity that is reflective and results in some profound change in internal consciousness. Brookfield insists that *true* self-directed learning must be associated with critical reflectivity.

Houle (1984) found patterns of education woven into the individual's life. He suggested five hypotheses that view education as:

1. The central purpose of life.
2. A means for reexamining life.
3. Only a part of a complex life.
4. Mastery of all knowledge.
5. A way of preserving and protecting the state.

Caffarella and O'Donnell disclaimed the Brookfield position faintly but suggested that empirical research grounded in contending philosophies needs to find some commonality upon which to build a coherent body of knowledge.

Comment

Typically, philosophical positions represent the values and belief systems of the philosophers. The reader is presented with a view of the universe as the philosopher prefers to see it — and as he or she wishes others might see it.

Thus, the Mezirow-Brookfield view restricts the concept of self-directed learning to reflective thinking and significant internal change, creating a rarified perspective with which most adult educators would struggle. If such is a requirement of true learning — self-directed or not — we must exclude most of what everyone knows. Also, we should then recognize that little such learning occurs intentionally or as a direct result of either traditional or self-directed education. Finally, it probably is impossible to confirm whether it has happened or not.

Such a definition probably renders the concept unresearchable and certainly beyond the expertise and competence of most adult educators. This definition defines self-directed learning as *thought* that defies observation and description. In contrast, describing self-directed learning as actively formulating goals and means in a traceable process provides questions that can be studied and answered.

Houle's (1984) addressing of philosophical positions suffers not from the specifics he requires but from too broad a perspective. His approach is dynamic as opposed to static but does not immediately conjure up research designs that would move his position forward.

Policy Issues

Policy issues, like philosophical positions, are mostly questions being raised in conceptual articles in the field of adult education. Caffarella and O'Donnell have suggested three basic questions that identify and separate policy issues.

> Conceptual articles on policy related to self-directed learning ask questions such as the following: What is the role of the adult educator? What are the involvement parameters for educational institutions? What does the concept of self-directed learning mean to society as a whole (p. 207)?

Specifics calling for study are: responses to learner needs; subject matter; settings; standards and quality; and satisfaction or dissatisfaction. Some ethical considerations have to do with *if* and *how much* adult educators should be involved and whether they should try to change or improve learners' goals.

Comment

Policies formulated in education and elsewhere are usually expressions of some institutions' or individuals' beliefs and mission preferences. Thus, policy making can be assumed to serve first the needs and desires of the policy makers.

Policies related to self-directed learning present a delicate issue because adult educators are likely to be intruders in a very private area where learners are by definition acting on their own behalf. Certainly, important ethical issues need to be resolved before policy is established.

Initially, it would seem that adult educators may be justified in only two roles. First, for those who believe self-directed learning is inherently beneficial, adult educators may become advocates, supporting it as they would any effort to which they are committed. Second, they can offer themselves as resources, ready to assist self-directed learners when and as requested. Very careful consideration should precede policy making related to other roles and issues.

Caffarella and O'Donnell conclude with a call for increased research in all their categories (with a tempered view of more verification studies) and exhorting the field to move forward in mature and sophisticated research designs and methodologies.

Summary

This article has maintained its value beyond historical interest in establishing categories that bring some order to a scattered body of literature. Indeed, many of the researchers were not aware of the work already done by their peers in the field and often made declarations that were plainly in error. Also, the categories are such that they have given direction to further studies, and future reviews must necessarily use this material as a launching point.

Since this paper appeared, a spate of books, articles, and monographs dealing with self-directed learning have been published and circulated broadly in the field. That flow seems to be accelerating. An annual international symposium has been held and its papers published since 1986. The list of new references, citations, and names being added to the field of research and conceptualizing in self-directed learning continues to grow at an amazing pace. Self-directed learning has indeed become the central area of interest in adult education during the past decade and promises to hold that dominance for the 1990s.

The reader of current literature should first be prepared to understand and appreciate the state-of-the-art in self-directed learning, by familiarity with this article by Rosemary S. Caffarella and Judith M. O'Donnell.

References

Boshier, R. (1983). *Adult learning projects research: An alchemist's fantasy.* Invited address to American Educational Research Association, Montreal.

Brockett, R. G. (1985). A response to Brookfield's critical paradigm of self-directed adult learning. *Adult Education Quarterly, 36*, 55-59.

Brockett, R. G. (1985a). Methodological and substantive issues in the measurement of self-directed learning readiness. *Adult Education Quarterly, 36*, 15-24.

Brookfield, S. D. (1981). Independent adult learning. *Studies in Education, 13*, 15-27.

Brookfield, S. D. (1984). Self-directed learning: A critical paradigm. *Adult Education Quarterly, 35*, 59-71.

Caffarella, R. S., & Caffarella, E. P. (1986). Self-directedness and learning contracts in adult education. *Adult Education Quarterly, 36*, 226-234.

Caffarella, R. S., & O'Donnell, J. M. (1987). Self-directed learning: A critical paradigm revisited. *Adult Education Quarterly, 37*, 199-211.

Coolican, P. M. (1974). Self-planned learning: Implications for the future of adult education. *Technical Report No. 74-507.* Syracuse, NY: Syracuse University, (ERIC Document No. ED 095 254).

Guglielmino, L. M. (1977). Development of the self-directed learning readiness scale. (Doctoral dissertation, University of Georgia). *Dissertation Abstracts International, 38*, 6467A

Houle, C. O. (1984). *Patterns of learning.* San Francisco, CA: Jossey Bass.

Kasworm, C. E. (1983). An examination of self-directed contract learning as an instructional strategy. *Innovative Higher Education, 8*(1), 45-54.

Knowles, M. S. (1975). *Self-directed learning.* NY: Association Press.

Mezirow, J. (1985). A critical theory of self-directed learning. In S. D. Brookfield (Ed.), *Self-directed learning; Theory and practice.* (New directions for Continuing Education, No. 25). San Francisco, CA: Jossey-Bass.

Mocker, D., & Spear, G. (1982). *Lifelong learning: Formal, informal, non-formal, and self-directed learning.* Kansas City: Center for Resource Development, University of Missouri-Kansas City. (ERIC Document No. ED 220 723).

Oddi, L. F. (1984). Development of an instrument to measure self-directed continuing learning. (Doctoral dissertation, Northern Illinois University, 1984). *Dissertation Abstracts International, 46,* 49A.

Oddi, L. F. (1986). Development and validation of an instrument to identify self-directed continuing learners. *Adult Education Quarterly, 36,* 97-107.

Penland, P. R. (1979). Self-initiated learning. *Adult Education, 29,* 170-179.

Spear, G. E., & Mocker, D. W. (1984). The organizing circumstance: Environmental determinants in self-directed learning. *Adult Education Quarterly, 35,* 1-10.

Torrance, E. P., & Mourad, S. (1978). Some creative and style of learning and thinking correlates of Guglielmino's self-directed learning readiness scale. *Psychological Reports, 43,* 1167-71.

Tough, A. (1971). *The adult's learning projects: A fresh approach to theory and practice in adult education.* Toronto, Ontario: The Ontario Institute for Studies in Education.

Tough, A. (1978). Major learning efforts: Recent research and future directions. *Adult Education, 28,* 250-263.

Tough, A. (1982). *Intentional changes: A fresh approach to helping people change.* Chicago, IL: Follett.

Chapter Thirteen

Self-Directed Learning:
Application and Theory

Malcolm S. Knowles on Huey Long and Associates

Dr. Knowles is Professor Emeritus of Adult Education. He is one of the most widely respected and published leaders in the field of adult education. His interest in self-directed learning has been an important stimulus to the field. His retirement from active faculty responsibilities has had the affect of freeing him to provide adult educators the kind of leadership that can only come from a senior statesperson.

This book is a collection of papers presented at the North American Symposium on Adult Self-Directed Learning, held in August of 1986, at the University of Georgia. The purpose of the symposium was to explore the "state of the art" regarding research, theory, and practice in self-directed learning. As the participants in the symposium were primarily university professors of adult and continuing education, about 90% of the papers are concerned with research and theory and 10% with practice or application.

Historical Perspective and Issues

In the opening chapter, "Self-Directed Learning Reconsidered," Huey Long puts the book in historical perspective and summarizes the main issues addressed in the subsequent 10 papers. He points out:

> Self-directed adult learning, as a human endeavor, is not a modern phenomenon. As a topic of scientific inquiry, it is. Traditionally, scholars of adult education trace the beginnings

of scientific inquiry into adult self-directed inquiry to Houle (1961) and his student Tough (1967). Thus, at least the majority of identified research and theory concerning the topic is less than two generations old (p. 1).

And in that period of time, he asserts, "There has been a rapidly expanding body of research and 'hortatory literature' on the subject." Long continues:

. . . despite the favorable conditions suggested by the popularity of the topic, adult self-directed learning remains weakly conceptualized, ill defined, inadequately studied, and tentatively comprehended (p. 1-2).

He summarizes the issues explored in subsequent chapters as follows:

1. Conceptualization of what adult self-directed learning is or is not, especially the meaning of the terms "self-directed" and "learning."
2. The direction and methodology of the research to date regarding the topic.
3. Barriers to the dissemination of research-based knowledge about self-directed learning and practical suggestions for its implementation.

Ambiguities

In Chapter Two, "Conceptual, Methodological, and Practical Ambiguities in Self-Directed Learning," Stephen Brookfield elaborates on the problem of definition of terms. Brookfield concludes:

Perhaps the most common programmatic format in higher and adult education is one in which self-directed and other-directed modes of educational decision-making are interrelated. There is a bargaining and negotiating process, through which the wishes, desires, interests, perceived needs and outright demands of the chief players (learners, teacher, administrators) interact in a transactional manner (p. 20).

He also expresses reservations about the over-reliance of much of the writing in this field on the philosophical orientation of humanistic psychologists, with an emphasis on process at the expense of content. He further proposes that a facilitator of learning must be concerned with both. Finally, he is quite critical of the skewed populations used in the research on self-directed learning and the reliance primarily on self-reports.

Regarding the implementation of self-directed learning in formal educational programs, Brookfield points out that one is likely to encounter many contradictions. For example, he asks:

> What happens when students accuse you of avoiding your professional duty and shirking your responsibility, because you refuse to prescribe for them the exact format of their activities? How do you convince faculty in other departments, not to mention your administration, that what you are doing does not reek of the charlatan approach of the degree mills, but is worthwhile?

And so on. He proposes that at least some of these criticisms can be lessened, if not avoided, by providing extensive and comprehensive preparation and training of the faculty and entering students (without specifying of what this preparation and training would consist). He also warns that one is likely to face institutional constraints, such as prescribed curricula; standardized grades; rigid time requirements; and imposed, uniform, evaluative criteria. He suggests that educators who choose to work in such tradition-bound institutions "must expect to encounter ambiguity, contradictions, and compromise in their efforts to promote self-directed learning." To some, Brookfield conjectures:

> The price will be too great to pay, given the limited benefits that accrue to learners when only a relatively small measure of self-directedness is introduced into programs. Others will continue to develop a high level of tolerance for ambiguity . . . They will pay a price in their professional and personal lives for this activity, but they will draw sustenance from other educators who are dealing with the same contradictions and compromises. They will also experience the exhilaration and euphoria exhibited by those whose attempts to conceive, plan and conduct their own learning result in significant changes in their self-esteem and an increased sense of their self-worth and individual capacity (pp. 32-33).

Finally, he raises two issues: the time-consuming nature of self-directed learning and the personal compatibility of learners and facilitators. He concludes:

Research and conceptual analysis of self-directed learning
is at a crucial point. Essentially, we can take one of two
directions. We can accept the general consensus that self-
directed learning is a uniquely adult form of learning, . . .
and that facilitating this form of learning is the unique
mission of educators of adults. Alternatively, we can
acknowledge that self-directed learning is far more complex, ambiguous, and fluid than had at first been imagined.
Knowing this, we can begin to encourage some open, hon-
est and heated debate concerning its conceptualization and
ways of researching the phenomenon.

He proposes that the second direction is, in the long term, "the
only way we will advance our conceptual and theoretical understanding of adult learning and the only way we will ever be taken seriously
as an academic field of study" (pp. 36-37).

Research and Trends

In Chapter Three, Rosemary Caffarella and Judith O'Donnell present an overview of "Research in Self-Directed Learning: Past,
Present, and Future Trends." They group the large number of studies
into five categories:

1.   Nature of the philosophical position of the researcher.
2.   Verification studies.
3.   Nature of the method of self-directed learning.
4.   Nature of the individual learner.
5.   Policy questions (the role of the educator, institutions, and
     society).

They find that verification studies:

. . . have consumed the bulk of the research effort, followed
closely by (and mostly in conjunction with) nature of the
method. More attention has been paid, especially in recent
years, to the nature of the individual learner. Little emphasis has been given to the nature of the philosophical position or basic policy questions (p. 40).

They conclude:

Self-directed learning is an important concept in adult education based on the number of research studies and conceptual articles. It appears to be an area where many of us

have cut our research teeth. We cannot yet draw tight conclusions about definitive findings. We can, however, draw
a net around the concept and conclude: that self-directed
learning does exist; that adults utilize a variety of methods
in their self-directed learning; that it appears to be beneficial to adult educators to have a better understanding of
the personal characteristics of individuals engaged in self-
directed learning; that we, as adult educators, are motivated by personal philosophies of adult education, and use
these philosophies to set normative parameters around the
self-directed learning concept; and that we are concerned
with our role in self-directed learning, concerned enough
to be calling for policies to guide our actions (p. 57).

Emphasis on Business and Industry

Chapter Six of this book, "Self-Directed Learning in Business and
Industry: An Information Age Imperative," by Lucy M. and Paul J.
Guglielmino, has a focus that may be of special interest to corporate
trainers and human resource developers. The tone of the chapter is
set in the opening sentences:

In a world where change is constant, self-directed learning
is a necessity. This is especially true in business and industry, where profitability depends on maintaining productivity and preventing obsolescence.

It then examines several factors that call for the development of
increased options for self-directed learning in business and industry,
including the impact of the Information Age, the impact of productivity improvement efforts, and the accelerating technological revolution.

It contains a major section on research on self-directed learning
in business and industry and gives detailed attention to the use of the
Guglielmino *Self-Directed Learning Readiness Scale.*

The authors close with a description of a proposed model for
training and development programs in business and industry that
involves the creation of learning resource centers that are easily
accessible to all employees. Case descriptions are given of several
such centers in corporations.

Other Contributions of the Book

The remaining seven chapters of Long's book explore the status of research into self-directed learning in particular institutional contexts or functional areas.

In Chapter Four, "Self-directed Learning in Institutional Contexts: An Exploratory Study of Adult Self-Directed Learners in Adult Education," Carol Kasworm suggests a perspective and supportive research study concerning self-directed learning within an institutional setting. She presents a conceptual framework for considering self-directed learning in relation to institutional or organizational strategies. She also suggests key principles, assumptions, and operational definitions for examining self-directed learning in this framework.

The findings of this research effort are reported under the headings (1) nature of the learner, (2) conditions for engaging in self-directed learning, (3) readiness to learn, (4) orientation to learn, (5) motivation to learn, (6) context and resources for self-directed learning, (7) processes in conducting self-directed learning, and (8) learning outcomes.

In Chapter Five, "Self-directed Learning: Individualizing Instruction," Roger Hiemstra describes why there is a need to individualize the instruction associated with adult learning, and he outlines the development and use of his Individualized Teaching Learning Process (ITLP). His position is based on the premise that the potentiality of humans as learners can only be maximized when there is a deliberate interaction between three elements: (1) learning process, (2) learning needs and interests, and (3) available instructional resources.

In Chapter Seven, "Improving Dissemination of Knowledge about Self-Directedness in Education," Robert Smith describes applications of self-directed learning knowledge and dissemination of that knowledge in programming and instruction. His work focuses on (1) what we know about educational knowledge and its dissemination, (2) potential users of self-directedness information, and (3) improvements in self-directed learning information.

In Chapter Eight, "Autodidactic Learning Experiences," Claudia Danis and Nicole Tremblay present the results of research conducted to review the prevailing adult learning principles. They do so by means of a comparison between the learning principles suggested by adult education experts and the corresponding propositions inferred from an analysis of the learning descriptions of self-taught adults recognized for their expertise in their respective fields of learning.

As a result of this study, Danis and Tremblay arrived at the following conclusions:

1. Various models of adult learning, as well as underlying concepts, are required to succeed in defining the components of an adult learning theory.
2. There are assumptions that are considered or formulated as principles on which a theory cannot be based.
3. An effort must be made to identify principles that are situated at an acceptable general level in a theory-building perspective and those that may present a strategic dimension relative to adult learning.
4. It will be necessary to verify the pertinence of the extrapolation that certain principles and elements that are characteristic of self-directed learning are also characteristic of adult learning in general.
5. Research centered on theory-building in adult education, requires the creation and testing of new methodologies adapted to desired goals.

In Chapter Nine, "Beyond the Organizing Circumstances: A Search for Methodology for the Study of Self-Directed Learning," George Spear reports on a continuation of an investigation he conducted with Donald Mocker (See Chapter Nine) into some aspects of the affects of the environment on the process and content of self-directed learning. This work explores possible relationships with certain theoretical bases and suggests implications of further study. Spear concluded:

1. The data tended to confirm the efficacy of the social learning theory approach and provided the suggestion that the proper means for studying self-directed learning is an analysis of clusters of interactive elements, rather than an analysis of the learning project as a whole.
2. Additional research is needed to test this approach to determine if it can lead to insights that add clarification to what is known about self-directed learning.

In Chapter Ten, "Self-directed Learning and Natural Language Processing," Patrick Penland discusses the need for the development of electronic telecommunications and computer technology to interface with the way self-directed learners think and process information, rather than in the way computers operate.

In Chapter Eleven, "Self-directed Learning Readiness: Assessment and Validation," Huey Long and Stephen Agyekum review research designed to assess and validate Guglielmino's *Self-Directed Learning Readiness Scale* (SDLRS). As a result of this review, they reached the following conclusions:

1. The research findings are generally supportive of the validity of the SDLRS, based on convergent and divergent associations between variables used in the unitary studies and a multi-trait, multi-methods analysis.
2. Item total score correlations may be adequate when the scale is used with a college-age sample similar to the one used by Guglielmino to develop the scale.

All these papers follow the issues and themes identified in the first three chapters to some degree. On the whole, they confirm their position that this is a field of research and application that is in the early stages of its evolution.

Summary

My own assessment is that this book makes a significant contribution to the issues with which future theorists and researchers need to be concerned. But I also believe that many practitioners of self-directed adult learning programs, particularly in non-traditional higher education, business and industry, adult basic education, religious adult education, and voluntary organizations, are considerably ahead of their academic colleagues in inventing ways to implement the concept of self-directed learning in real programs. I can't help but wish that the North America Symposium on Self-Directed Learning had included a larger representation of practitioners.

Implications for Trainers

However, the concerns noted above notwithstanding, there are important implications for practice suggested by several of the papers:

1. Prepare your system for experimenting with self-directed learning by: exposing the administrators and faculty to relevant literature; providing orientation seminars or workshops for learners; conducting seminars or workshops for faculty on the skills for facilitating self-directed learners; providing multiple options for learners at different points on the continuum of readiness for self-directed learning; and establishing an evaluation process based on evidence of competency-development rather than norm-referenced grading.

2. Provide learners with access to both human and material learn-
    ing resources, at times and places that are convenient for adults
    with such life commitments as families, jobs, and civic responsi-
    bilities.
3. Provide flexible time schedules for activities that take into
    account these life commitments.
4. Provide an adequate support system, including peer-helping
    groups, faculty consultation, and community volunteers.

References

Houle, C. O. (1961). *The inquiring mind.* Madison, WI: The University of
    Wisconsin Press.

Long, H. B. & Associates. (1988). *Self-directed learning: Application and
    Theory.* Athens, GA: Adult Education Department, University of Georgia.

Tough, A. M. (1967). *Learning without a teacher.* Toronto, Ontario: The
    Ontario Institute for Studies in Education.

Chapter Fourteen

Self-Directed Learning: Emerging Theory and Practice

Nicole A. Tremblay on Huey Long and Associates

Dr. Tremblay is Associate Professor of Andragogy at the University of Montreal. She began her research into self-directed learning in 1981 with her doctoral dissertation, which involved a study of help and assistance among self-taught adults. She has worked with Claudia Danis in joint studies of autodidaxy and is presently researching self-directed learning strategies in the workplace.

Studies have shown that most learning activities in the workplace are conducted through an informal/self-directed mode. Training budgets, however, are allocated mostly for formal/other-directed activities. This situation urges those involved in human resource development to reappraise ongoing policies and explore new training opportunities.

This chapter is a synthesis of a book titled *Self-Directed Learning: Emerging Theory and Practice* by Huey B. Long and his associates. It deals with four important concerns in the field of self-directed learning:

1. The notion of *project* and its historical dimension.
2. The definition of *self-directed learning* and its conceptualization.
3. The *measurement* of self-directedness in learning and the validity and reliability of the actual tests.
4. The *implementation* of educational settings that can facilitate self-directed learning.

As you may have observed, theoretical and methodological aspects of self-directed learning predominate over more practical ones. This synthesis will thus provide an opportunity to name, describe, and classify different aspects of the "beast" in order to better define its usefulness.

Historical Dimensions of Self-Directed Learning

Independent study and inquiry have always been useful strategies to gain knowledge or acquire skills as parents, citizens, and workers. Johnstone and Rivera's (1965) national survey in the sixties indicated that these strategies were common and important in adulthood. At the end of the same decade, Tough (see Chapters 6, 7 and 8) gave the first operational definition of the phenomenon he called "self-planned learning." His work allowed thousands of researchers to verify, in their own country and with a variety of adults, that self-planned projects were numerous and important. Guglielmino (1977) and Spear and Mocker (1984) (Chapter 9) made other important contributions to this growing field of research, by developing an instrument to measure self-direction and by developing the notion of organizing circumstances in self-directed learning projects, respectively.

As a young and fast-growing body of research, however, the fundamental notion of self-directed learning calls for more clarity. As pointed out by Charlene Sexton, "Scholars have noted the inadequate conceptualization in this body of research" (1989). Further, she suggests an historical perspective can be considered as a relevant means of overcoming ambiguities surrounding the phenomenon of self-directed learning.

Sexton suggests that the roots of self-directed learning theory are partially found in the project method and child-centered foci in American curriculum theory, as exemplified in the work of William Heard Kilpatrick (1918). Kilpatrick was concerned about identifying educational methods promoting coherent practice. He tried to find the unifying concept of education and practice, calling it a "project." All those who have concerns for professional and continuing education will acknowledge the importance of Kilpatrick's preoccupation.

For both Kilpatrick in the field of pedagogy, and Tough in the field of andragogy, the notion of project encompasses a wide variety of activities (observing, listening, discussing) that are conducted for a variety of purposes (solving daily life problems, gaining general knowledge, etc.). Tough and Kilpatrick suggest that a learning process evolves around four major steps: purposing, planning, executing, and judging. Furthermore, both writers consider that a highly deliberate effort, a wholehearted activity, or an intentional change are the underpinnings of a learning project. Their definitions emphasize the fact that learning is not merely an incidental affair and that it requires a high degree of self-direction on the part of the learner. This criterion gives more credibility to informal strategies and is considered of less value in more formal settings.

Self-direction is considered the focus of the very notion of project. Self-direction is also the focus of learning in adulthood as described by Knowles (1970) in *The Modern Practice of Adult Education*, a seminal work in the field of adult education:

> But something dramatic happens to his self-concept when an individual defines himself as an adult . . . His self-concept becomes that of a self-directing personality (p. 40).

The fundamental notions of freedom, autonomy, and self-directedness have been taken into account by both founders and leaders in the field of adult education. Houle, Knowles, and Tough in the sixties and seventies held that self-directedness is central to learning and that it is a key element for our understanding of learning in adulthood. The founders of the New School of Social Research, at the beginning of the century, had initiated the Adult Education Movement. They deeply believed that adults are able to learn and that the humanization of knowledge and the democracy of culture would ensure social and individual autonomy and growth.

These general considerations on self-direction in learning are quite far from our daily worries about learning and training. But it is also important for us, as practitioners, to have larger views of what is and what could become self-directed learning. It is not a peripheral phenomenon in adult education, which deals solely with methodological and technical aspects of learning. This is not a mere trend destined to disappear in the near future. Self-directed learning is an important fact, indissociable from learning itself and intimately connected with adult learning specifically.

Defining Self-Direction in Learning

Self-directed learning encompasses a variety of learning and teaching strategies and methods. The reality depicted by the notion of self-directedness refers to the "self-made person" whose life is a successful long-term learning project, as well as to the student who has registered for a course that makes use of open, pedagogical techniques, such as learning contracts.

As Brookfield (1985) pointed out (see Chapter 10), a variety of terms are used to define a number of realities in the field of self-directed learning. Sometimes the same term refers to many aspects of the phenomenon and sometimes many terms are used to name the same reality. This semantical wavering can be explained by the relative newness of the study of self-directed learning. Different terms such as "independent study or inquiry," "experiential learning," "distance education," "self-planned learning projects," "self-directed learning," "self-instruction," or "individualized learning" are used to define the many facets of self-directed learning. Furthermore, self-directed learning can take place in a variety of formal and informal educational settings. As suggested by Bonham (l989), it seems impractical right now to attempt a definition that would be so broad as to include all instances in which the term might be used.   One of the most exciting challenges in the coming years will be to lay out a typology of learning in self-directed learning situations and to propose a glossary of terms related to self-direction.

High Psychological Control

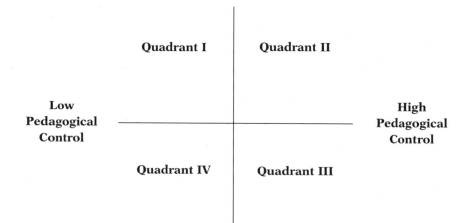

Low Psychological Control

Figure 14.1 An illustration of the relationship between pedagogical and psychological control in self-directed learning.*

*Reprinted from Long (l989) with permission.

According to Long (l989), the concept of self-directedness can be defined on different levels:

1.   On a social level that refers to some kind of isolation of the learner.

2.   On a pedagogical level where the learner has to identify his/her learning needs, organize a strategy, and gain the resources.
3.   On a psychological level that refers to the mental activity of the learner.

Long considers that the social and pedagogical levels are less important than the psychological dimension. For him, the critical element for defining self-direction is the amount of freedom the learner has to influence the pedagogical process, i.e., self-directed learning happens only when learners primarily control their learning processes. Psychological freedom and control are the standard criteria for identifying a self-directed learning activity. In practice, this means that a formal classroom situation can be as self-directed as a distance education course, an individualized instruction kit, or an independent study.

Long proposes a model of self-directed learning that involves the learner in group activity. It refers to educational settings, such as classrooms or structured workshops. It takes into account the psychological and pedagogical aspects of the relationship as shown in figure 14.1.

This model can be very useful in describing the kind of pedagogical situation that is relevant to different degrees of self-direction of participants. Long's model suggests that more self-direction will occur in the situation described by Quadrant I, where the learner has high psychological control and the teacher makes use of low control teaching strategies. Less self-direction will happen in Quadrant III, where the learner has low psychological control and the teacher uses high pedagogical control. The model also suggests that the likelihood of a learner dropping out is probably greatest under the conditions represented by Quadrant II, where there is high psychological control on the part of the learner and high pedagogical control on the part of the teacher. It is likely that personal learner dissatisfaction will be high in both Quadrants II and IV, where the level of psychological control competes with the level of pedagogical control.

This model presents essential aspects practitioners should always consider when organizing learning activities. That is, how can the general characteristics of my activity match the general characteristics of the learner for whom it has been designed? It would be of great interest to consider systematically this fundamental aspect at the early stages of any planning. The dimensions of Long's model may serve as general criteria for the orientation of learning designs.

Garrison (1989) also refers to the notion of control as the central characteristic of self-direction in learning, and he suggests that control is "concerned with the opportunity and ability to influence,

direct, and determine decisions related to the educational process"
(p. 56). The definition is interesting because it takes into account, on
the one hand, the educational context that may become an opportunity and, on the other hand, the competencies of the learner who may
have the ability to seize these opportunities and make good use of
them. Garrison insists that autonomy or freedom remains an empty
concept without intellectual, attitudinal, and dispositional proficiency on the part of the learner and good resources on the part of
the educational setting. Figure 14.2 presents the model proposed by
Garrison.

Control is the central part of this model. The three essential
dimensions of control are independence (on the part of the pedagogical design), proficiency (on the part of the learner), and support (on
the part of the environment). The model also takes into account the
three dimensions of an educational activity: (1) the content of the
activity, (2) the learner, and (3) the teacher who participates in the
process. The control is shared between learner and teacher. In a self-
directed learning context the teacher or facilitator might simply provide information and guidance. Garrison states that there is no
contradiction in receiving help and remaining in control. It has been
demonstrated that highly self-directed learners find assistance from a
great number and variety of materials and human resources in their
immediate environment.

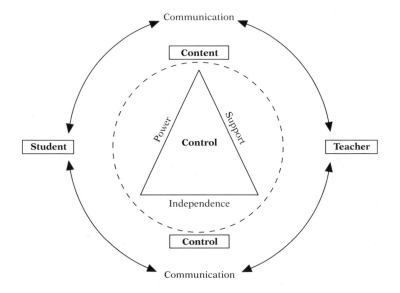

Figure 14.2 Control and the educational transaction.*

*Reprinted from Garrison (1989) with permission

Garrison's model is presented in a communication process called the "transactional educational process." The transactions between teacher and learner and between the individual and the learning context operate during planning stages of an activity, as well as during late instructional phases. This model has been developed in a distance education perspective, but it is also relevant for self-directed learning in general.

Continuing education now appears to be a means to adjust to a world where change seems to be the only lasting reality. Self-directed learning strategies can be considered relevant and well-adapted to this changing world. As practitioners in the field of training and adult education, we must act creatively in proposing new educational alternatives to workers and citizens. Human resource managers must strive to facilitate transition to greater self-direction in learning. Self-direction will not be well served, however, if we throw out all structures. On the contrary, it takes good planning and well-organized structures to implement innovative learning strategies. Learners call for support to operate safely and to enjoy controlling their learning endeavors.

Measuring Self-Direction in Learning

As shown in figure 14.1, Long suggests that self-direction in learning has both pedagogical and psychological dimensions. The psychological dimension of self-direction raises important questions:

1. What are the main characteristics one should possess to be an effective self-directed learner?
2. What kinds of skills and what types of personalities are typical of self-directed learners?
3. How can we ensure that one will be a good self-directed learner?
4. Is it possible to enhance someone's self-directedness?

In short, is self-direction a learning style? According to Bonham (1989), self-directed learning acts as a learning style. She defines a learning style as:

A way of acting and thinking in a learning situation: the person feels comfortable with that approach and possesses any skills necessary for using it; where there is a choice the person chooses this approach (p. 14).

There are three reasons to consider self-directed learning a learning style. First, a number of learning style instruments have elements or subcategories related to autonomy or independence as part of what they measure, and these instruments are reliable and have been validated repeatedly. Second, there is evidence in the literature that self-directedness is treated as a style by authors. Finally, there is some experimental evidence of self-directed learning acting as a style. For example, researchers established correlations between the level of self-direction of an individual and the quantity of self-directed projects he/she initiates and the time he/she devotes to them. Other researchers found that high scores on the *Self-Directed Learning Readiness Scale* (Guglielmino, 1977) correspond to facility in planning, organizing, conducting, and evaluating a learning project.

The Self-Directed Learning Readiness Scale

This instrument is the first attempt that has ever been made to measure self-directed learning. Guglielmino developed her instrument as a way of measuring an individual's potential for self-directed learning. It has been used in many studies. The test presents 58 items to be answered on a five-level, Likert-type scale. It exists in many versions and has been translated into many languages.

Guglielmino applied a factor analysis to her findings and obtained eight categories that describe a self-directed learner:

1. Openness to learning opportunities.
2. Self-concept as an effective learner.
3. Initiative and independence in learning.
4. Informed acceptance of responsibility for one's own learning.
5. Love of learning.
6. Creativity.
7. Future orientation.
8. Ability to use basic study and problem-solving skills.

Inferring from the results of her survey, Guglielmino draws this portrait of a highly self-directed learner:

1. One who exhibits initiative, independence, and persistence in learning.
2. One who accepts responsibility for his or her own learning and views problems as challenges, not obstacles.
3. One who is capable of self-discipline and has a high degree of curiosity.
4. One who has a strong desire to learn or change and is self-confident.

5. One who is able to develop a plan for completing work, to use basic study skills, to organize his or her time, and to set an appropriate pace for learning.
6. One who enjoys learning and has a tendency to be goal-oriented.

Self-Directed Learning and Associated Factors

More than a 150 studies have used the *Self-Directed Learning Readiness Scale*. Self-directedness has been associated with a large variety of factors. It seems important to present the more significant of these correlations here. Self-directedness has been linked with sociological, demographical, psychological, organizational, and educational factors.

There is no evidence that self-direction has any correlation with age, sex, or ethnicity; it varies according to activity or methodology. But some correlations have been established between self-direction and scholarship that tend to indicate that those who went to school for a longer period had acquired basic tools necessary to be an effective learner. This suggests that learning methods acquired in school are transferred (and are transferable) and that those tools are pre-requisites to conduct effective, self-directed learning projects.

Psychological factors have been related to self-direction in learning in more than 50% of the studies. Correlations have been established between self-direction in learning and right-brain preference, creativity, and divergent style, as identified in *Kolb's Learning Style Inventory*. Learners who display these styles tend to prefer observation to action, intuition to more deductive strategies, and a holistic approach to a well-planned, linear mode. Many authors reported correlations between field-independence and self-direction. This may suggest that highly self-directed learners rely less on well-structured and formal learning activities and may prefer minimally restrictive educational environments. Bonham (1989) suggests that it is possible that these individuals exhibit hostility or panic when they are expected to produce specific goals and plans too early in the learning process.

Some studies conducted in the workplace indicate correlations between the SDLRS and the *Work Environment Scale*, (WES). Self-direction in learning shows a correlation with subtests of the WES, such as orientation to future, creativity, and competencies in problem solving. SDLRS scores have been correlated with results of the *Adult Learning Project Interview Schedule*. Strong correlations are reported between the SDLRS and the number of hours an employee devotes to self-planned projects and to the number of projects he/she conducts. Other studies show correlations between self-direction and scholarship as found in other populations, but findings vary according to job performance or hierarchical status.

Validation of the SDLRS

McCune (1988) made a unique and important contribution to the work of Guglielmino. She conducted a meta-analytic study of the SDLRS, aiming at a generalization of the instrument. Applying the Schmidt and Hunter methodology to the analysis of 67 studies that had made use of the SDLRS, McCune came to the conclusion that:

> The present study indicates a moderate but definite relationship between total SDLRS score and degree of involvement in self-directed learning activity. The results of this analysis lend strong support to the continued use of the SDLRS as a valid predictor of involvement in self-directed learning (p. 8).

The Oddi Continuing Learning Inventory (OCLI)

Lorys Oddi (1986) was interested in identifying the personality characteristics of those who would engage in continuing learning in their profession. She reviewed the literature and found personality traits that characterize the self-directed learner. These traits have been grouped into three dimensions, which she has defined as follows:

1. *Proactive Drive versus Reactive Drive:* Individuals who possess a high self-esteem and self-confidence. These individuals have self-regulating behaviors and can engage in a self-initiated and sustained activity that is directed toward a high-level goal. At the opposite are individuals who tend to discontinue activities when facing obstacles, exhibit low self-confidence, and rely on others to stimulate learning.
2. *Cognitive Openness versus Defensiveness:* Individuals who are open to new ideas, adapt to change, and have tolerance for ambiguity. Their counterpart is an individual who is rigid, fears failure, and avoids new ideas.
3. *Commitment to Learning versus Apathy or Aversion to Learning:* Individuals who have positive attitudes about engaging in a variety of learning activities and have a preference for thought-provoking, leisure games. The opposite is hostile attitudes towards engaging in learning.

The OCLI has not been used as frequently as the SDLRS. In general, the personality traits described by Oddi are similar to the characteristics of a self-directed learner as presented by Guglielmino. There is some consensus on the essential characteristics of self-directed learners.

Validation of the OCLI

Oddi tried to estimate the construct validity of her instrument. Her study addressed the following questions:

1. Is there a relationship between total scores on the OCLI and the number of continuing education programs voluntarily attended by registered nurses?
2. Is there a relationship between total scores on the OCLI and those on the *Job Activity Survey* (JAS)? The JAS is designed to measure frequency of participation in on-the-job activities.
3. Is there a relationship between the OCLI and subscales of the JAS in learning modes such as inquiry, instruction, and performance?

Oddi concludes that the significant, positive relationship she observed between total scores on the OCLI and total scores on the JAS indicates convergent validity of the OCLI as a measure of self-directed learning among nurses who have been studied. She suggests that another study should be directed toward the refinement of items, in order to measure better learning that occurs through inquiry, instruction, and performance modes.

Criticism of the Validity of the SDLRS and OCLI

Definitions proposed by Guglielmino and Oddi indicate that the opposite of a self-directed learner is someone who has no initiative; has no persistence in learning; views problems as obstacles; and lacks curiosity, enjoyment of learning, and basic study skills. Bonham (1989) makes an important point in her rigorous analysis of the construct of self-direction. She says that the true opposite that lurks in the background of these definitions is the non-learner. In that perspective, the *Self-Directed Learning Readiness Scale* and the *Oddi Continuing Learning Inventory* seem to measure a propensity for learning in general and not a propensity for self-directed learning specifically. The characteristics listed by the two researchers define an enthusiastic learner and not a self-directed learner as opposed to an other-directed learner. As Bonham puts it:

> The SDLRS and OCLI seem designed to discover the person who likes to learn in any setting . . . the instruments do little to distinguish among avid learners, those who prefer self-directedness and those who prefer something else (p. 23).

Bonham submits a model distinguishing between non-learners and learners, and between other-directed and self-directed learners (see figure 14.3).

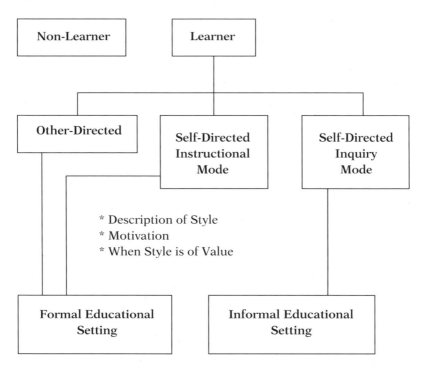

Figure 14.3 Proposed model for a learning style construct.*

*Adapted from Bonham (1989)

Criticism plays an important role in evaluating tests and other instruments of measure. Bonham's criticism of the SDLRS and the OCLI represents a major contribution to this trend of research because it calls for clarification of the concept of self-directedness. Indeed, an effective strategy to gain clarity is to oppose related concepts — such as self-directed and other-directed learning. Because self-directed learning encompasses a variety of learning situations (from the student in the classroom to the self-taught adult), it lacks specificity. Instruments designed to measure it will logically lack specificity.

Despite the fact that criticism has been addressed regarding the validity of the construct of the SDLRS and the OCLI, these instruments remain valid as established by McCune and Oddi. An important point is that these instruments seem to measure enthusiasm for learning — and it can be as important to have a measure of enthusiasm as one of self-directedness. These instruments have not been developed to predict who will have success in self-directed learning projects, or who can be selected as an effective self-directed employee, but they could help in establishing learning profiles or portraits.

Bridging Theory and Practice

Judith Klippel DeJoy and Helen Mills (1989) presented and analyzed an ongoing, educational program that is based on several self-directed learning principles and offers a range of services to a variety of adult learners. The Georgia Center for Continuing Education opened in 1957, under the auspices of a W. K. Kellogg Foundation grant. In 1984, a Personal Adult Learning Lab was created to provide a learning environment for facilitating self-directed learning. In developing this Center, those involved went through the following general steps:

Step 1: Developing the goals of the Learning Lab

The authors report that the Goals were developed:

1. To facilitate the self-directed learning process through the use of on-site staff.
2. To provide a variety of self-directed, instructional materials for individual use.
3. To provide a physical locale furnished with the necessary educational technology for delivering individualized instruction.
4. To extend the limitations of time and space, by providing access to materials and other resources at a distance, via communications technology.
5. To observe and record the characteristics of adult Learning Lab users, their interests, choices, and evaluations of their particular, self-directed learning experiences.

Step 2: Identifying Design Elements

The design elements included client populations, particular materials to be used, learning delivery modes, and the learning environment.

Adult learning principles developed by Knowles (1970) served as guidelines in the experiment. According to Knowles, an adult moves toward independence or self-directedness and tends to approach learning with a rich experience. The adult is interested primarily in immediate application and problem solving. Another principle taken into account was that adults are more or less ready to learn, depending on their developmental life stage. Another step was the identification of future clients of the Learning Lab. The founders established that it may be designed both for the population surrounding the campus, for academic faculty and staff, and for conferees who attend the Georgia Center for Continuing Professional Education.

Step 3: Establishing a Learning Environment

A survey was conducted to specify the particular instructional resources and delivery modes the Lab should offer. This survey asked future clients to identify the content areas they were interested in and the type of resources that would be suitable to them. The most attractive contents for potential clients were management and communications skills, computer training, and career exploration. According to essential aspects of self-directed modes of learning, the resources were self-instructional and self-paced. They do not require excessive computer or typing skills. Learning resources have been offered in several different delivery modes: computer-assisted instructional packages, videotapes, audiocassettes, self-assessment instruments, and manuals. The Learning Lab has an interactive video training workstation where interactive video introductory courses are offered.

The learning environment was developed in accordance with Tough's and Knowles' characteristics of an atmosphere conducive to self-directed learning. The physical environment was designed to promote a sense of privacy, to provide physical comfort, and to support learning with the presence of a trained facilitator. This facilitator helps in identifying appropriate materials and resources and in recognizing the value of what is already known by learners. This latter aspect seems important because some individuals surveyed expressed genuine doubt about their ability to make their own learning choices and evaluations. A good facilitator can encourage, stimulate, and persuade learners to carry on.

An analysis of the Learning Lab experiment led DeJoy and Mills to the identification of four general principles for the development of self-directed learning opportunities.

Principle #1. The content and subject matter of adult learning resources should reflect the documented interests and needs of the specific population served.

Principle #2. In support of individualized learning strategies, instructional resources should offer opportunities for the self-directed learner to control-manipulate-shape information to fit his/her personal learning style. For example:

a. Opportunities to practice new learning immediately.
b. Feedback on performance at regular intervals.
c. Adjustable levels of difficulty.
d. Adjustable pace of presentation.
e. Control of the sequence of information presentation.
f. Opportunity to review/correct/repeat information.
g. Opportunity to exit and reenter program without repetition.
h. Opportunity to save responses for future use.

Principle #3. The instructional design features of learning resources should contribute to the presentation of information in such a way as to enhance (not detract from) the learner's ability to process and assimilate the information:

a. Information should be presented in more than one format (e.g., watching, hearing, reading).
b. Displays (such as screens) should be easy to read, with an appropriate number of words and graphic images.
c. Color and graphics should support, rather than distract from, the information.
d. Instructions should be clear, and the learner should know how to respond.
e. Selection of options should be easy to understand and execute.
f. Presented information and any support material should be fully integrated.

Principle #4. The presence of a competent facilitator can contribute to the quality of the self-directed learning experience.

The first principle reiterates the need to understand the specific population involved in the self-directed learning experiences. It is important to survey their learning interests, requirements, and predispositions. This way of proceeding can save time, money, and energy. This principle has been pointed out by Knowles in 1970:

It is almost universally predictable that programs that are
based mostly on what somebody thinks people ought to
learn will fail . . . So in andragogy the starting point in program planning is always the adults' interests (p. 79).

Those engaged in building new experiences for adults must be
reminded of the highly voluntary nature of adult education.

The second principle presents a tenet of education: Individuals
learn with their own personal style, intelligence, experience, perception, etc. It follows that the embedded features of any particular
learning resource will influence the learning process. It is important
for learners to have some control over the material so they can per-
sonalize their learning. It should be possible for learners to adjust
pace of presentation and level of difficulty while controlling the
sequences of information. Self-directed learning resources should
provide opportunities to review and correct information and to exit
and reenter the program. According to experience and observations
by DeJoy and Mills, it is important for resources to give periodic feedback and offer immediate opportunities to practice new learning.

The third principle refers to often overlooked criteria that can
serve as a guideline when choosing or buying materials. Before making a decision one may ask: Does it allow learners to watch, hear,
and read? Do graphics and illustrations support or distract from
information? Are instructions and options clear? These very basic
questions may sometimes be completed by asking learners or future
learners to give their opinions on materials.

The fourth principle points out the importance of a facilitator.
The most important skill he/she must have is to recognize the current
perspective of the client and match descriptions to that perspective.
The facilitator must have the ability to encourage some level of self-
directed activity, particularly when an adult seems hesitant or presents little self-confidence. Many studies in distance education have
shown that situations with facilitators were more successful than
those merely providing technical support.

University of Georgia's Personal Adult Learning Lab provides
many interesting elements that may lead to the creation of other
learning centers, particularly in the workplace. Other experiments in
self-directed learning are being conducted in business and industry
across North America. Some of these have been applied in a systematic manner, but the results of most experiments remain to be more
generalized. It is important to think in terms of analyzing self-
directed learning experiments, in order to provide the field of adult
education with models leading to a more effective practice.

Conclusion

Theoretical aspects that have been presented in this chapter are important for progress in the field of self-directed learning. Authors address the essential question: "What is self-directed learning?" The concept seems to have gained in clarity during the past decade. Self-directed learning as a psychological characteristic has been differentiated from self-directed learning as a methodology. The notion of control has been emphasized as a central aspect of self-directedness. Criticism of the two instruments, which aim at measuring self-directedness, has called for a definition that takes into account other-directed learning.

Efforts to define a reality can only lead to a better grasp of its various components. Though some may dismiss these attempts as intellectual gymnastics, a better understanding of self-directed learning activities and their underlying principles may enlighten those working in educational settings as to ways of making better use of available resources. If most learning activities in the workplace are self-directed in nature, and if self-directed learning is among the best ways to update work-related skills, then it is indeed a small luxury to allow time for these theoretical considerations. Such an investment will inevitably pay off as new and innovative, self-directed learning practices emerge.

References

Bonham, L. A. (1989). Self-directed orientation toward learning: A learning style. In H. B. Long & Associates, *Self-directed learning: Emerging theory & practice* (pp. 13-42). Norman, OK: Oklahoma Research Center for Continuing Professional and Higher Education.

Brookfield, S. D. (1985). *Self-directed learning: From theory to practice.* (New Directions for Continuing Education, Number 25.) San Francisco, CA: Jossey-Bass.

DeJoy, J. K., & Mills, H. (1989). Bridging theory and practice: Applications in the development of services for self-directed learners. In H. B. Long & Associates, *Self-directed learning: Emerging theory & practice* (pp. 99-111). Norman, OK: Oklahoma Research Center for Continuing Professional and Higher Education.

Garrison, D. R. (1989). Facilitating self-directed learning: Not a contradiction in terms. In H. B. Long & Associates, *Self-directed learning: Emerging theory & practice* (pp. 53-62). Norman, OK: Oklahoma Research Center for Continuing Professional and Higher Education.

Guglielmino, L. M. (1977). Development of the self-directed learning readiness scale. (Doctoral dissertation, University of Georgia.) *Dissertation Abstracts International, 38,* 6467A.

Johnstone, J. W. and Rivera, R. J. (1965). *Volunteers for learning: A study of the educational pursuits of American adults.* Chicago, IL: Aldine Publishing Company.

Kilpatrick, W. H. (1918). The project method. *Teachers College Record, 19,* 319-35.

Knowles, M. (1970). *The modern practice of adult education: Andragogy versus pedagogy.* NY: Association Press.

Long, Huey B. (1989). Self-directed learning: Emerging theory and practice. In H.B. Long & Associates, *Self-directed learning: Emerging theory & practice* (pp. 1-11). Norman, OK: Oklahoma Research Center for Continuing Professional and Higher Education.

McCune, S. (1988). A meta-analytic study of adult self-direction in learning: A review of the research from 1977 to 1987. (Doctoral dissertation, Texas A&M University.) *Dissertation Abstracts International, 49,* 11A.

Oddi, L. F. (1986). Development and validation of an instrument to identify self-directed continuing learners. *Adult Education Quarterly, 36*(2), 97-107.

Sexton, C. (1989). The contribution of W. H. Kilpatrick's work (1918) to adult self-directed learning. In H. B. Long & Associates, *Self-directed learning: Emerging theory & practice* (pp. 113-123). Norman, OK: Oklahoma Research Center for Continuing Professional and Higher Education.

Spear, G. E., & Mocker, D. W. (1984). The organizing circumstance: Environmental determinants in self-directed learning. *Adult Education Quarterly, 35,* 1-10.

Chapter Fifteen

Advances in Research and Practice in Self-Directed Learning

Claudia Danis on Huey Long and Associates

Dr. Danis is Associate Professor of Andragogy at the University of Montreal. Before undertaking her academic career she worked primarily in the field of non-formal adult education in Latin America. Over the last fifteen years she has been focusing her research efforts on individual and collective adult self-directed learning processes.

Advances in Research and Practice in Self-Directed Learning is based on selected papers that were presented by international experts at the Third North American Symposium on Adult Self-Directed Learning. This original work deals with various topics that may prove to be most useful to educators, trainers, managers, and executives who are called upon to support and contribute to continuing adult education in the workplace. This work reflects the diversity of current research and practice in the field of self-directed learning.

The Experts' Various Perspectives

The contributors to this volume have studied the self-directed learning phenomenon from different perspectives. Some contributors have discussed the nature of the self-directed learning concept as such. Others have analyzed the main ideological orientations that influence both its practice and theory. Still others have mostly focused on various practical elements regarding the learning-teaching process of the educators or the individual adult learners.

Nature of the Self-Directed Learning Concept

Huey B. Long, in "Changing Concepts of Self-Direction in Learning," observes that researchers should discard many earlier reductionist conceptualizations and build a more complex and inclusive model of the self-directed learning phenomenon. In a theory-building perspective, this model should take into account the contingency and interaction of various essential factors such as the environment, the information available, the learner, his/her learning process, as well as the outcomes.

Peter Jarvis, in "Self-Directed Learning and the Theory of Adult Education," after having defined the two basic concepts of *self-directedness* and *learning,* proposes a multivariate model of the learning process that should distinguish between *self-directed* and *other-directed* learning. The model's nine major elements are the following: disjuncture, decision to learn, type of participation, aims and objectives, content, method, thought/language, assessment, and action/outcome.

Philip C. Candy, in "The Transition from Learner-Control to Autodidaxy: More Than Meets the Eye," first differentiates between self-directedness defined as a self-instructional process and self-directedness defined as a goal in itself. He then refers to the major notions of control of the instructional transaction and assistance obtained by the learner, in order to distinguish the many types of self-directed learning that range from *independent study* in formal educational settings to *autodidaxy* in informal, natural settings. Finally, with regard to future research, Candy recommends an interpretive approach rather than the dominant positivist approach.

Ideological Orientations

Lorraine S. Gerstner, in "On the Theme and Variations of Self-Directed Learning," explores the concept of self-directed learning from four philosophical perspectives: progressivist, humanist, behaviorist, and critical. These ideological orientations are compared and contrasted with regard to the interrelated concepts of selfhood, experience, education, and learning.

John M. Peters, in "Analysis of Practical Thinking in Self-Directed Learning," analyzes the dynamics of the relationship between self-directed learning and practical thinking from a problem-solving perspective. He particularly analyzes one adult's problem-related, self-directed learning experiences that were identified by means of his Action-Reason-Thematic Technique (ARTT).

Mark Dorsey, Roger Manning and Tom Shindell, in "Action Science as a Paradigm for a Critical Theory of Self-Directed Learning," suggest that adult educators and facilitators of self-directed learning use action science, a reflective theory that is centered on critical reflection, in order to improve their own practice. The authors relate action science to the instrumental, dialogic, and self-reflective functions of Mezirow's critical theory of self-directed learning. They finally describe the results of their empirical investigation into the possibility of increasing graduate students' consciousness regarding their self-directedness as individual learners.

Practical Elements

Huey B. Long and Stephen K. Agyekum, in "Toward a Theory of Self-Directed Learning: An Appraisal of Gibbons' Principles and Strategies," summarize Gibbons' 14 self-directed learning principles and their corresponding teaching strategies. The authors particularly examine three of these principles and strategies with regard to their instructive value within formal as well as informal educational settings and with regard to their theory-building potential. Gibbons and his colleagues studied the biographies of 20 self-taught experts in the fields of administration, science, letters, entertainment and invention.

Lorraine A. Cavaliere, in "The Wright Brothers as Self-Directed Learners: The Role and Relation of Goal Setting, Feedback and Motivation During the Process of Their Self-Directed Learning Project," analyzes from biographical and historical data bases the Wright brothers' self-directed learning process and learning behaviors in relation to their invention of the airplane. The author focuses on contextual forces such as the information networks and resources that were available in the inventors' informal educational setting.

Robert E. Nolan, in "Self-Direction in Adult Second Language Learning," focuses on the adult's second language learning process. The author discusses the paradoxical relationship between learner dependency and autonomy with regard to the acquisition of a prestructured learning content within such a formal educational setting.

Angela Sgroi, in "The Drive to Learn: Self-Directed Learning in a Formal Institutional Setting," also studies the adult's self-directed learning process with regard to the acquisition of a prestructured learning content (dance) within a formal institutional setting. In this author's investigation, the teacher-learner interaction emerged as an essential component of the learning process.

Gbolagade Adekanmbi, in "The Concept of Distance in Self-Directed Learning," identifies five main forms of distance or gaps with regard to the self-directed learner's situation, mainly within the structured setting of distance education. These five *distances* are physical, social, temporal, pedagogical, and public. The author subsequently proposes modalities for bridging those gaps.

Joanne Lambert and Jeannie Rountree-Wyly, in "Self-Directed Learners: Women Climbing the Corporate Ladder," carried out case studies of four upwardly mobile career women who trained themselves through both formal and informal self-directed learning efforts.

Sandra McCune, Lucy M. Guglielmino and Gonzalo Garcia, Jr., in "Adult Self-Direction in Learning: A Meta-Analytic Study of Research using the *Self-Directed Learning Readiness Scale*," analyze 29 empirical studies of adult self-direction in learning that used Guglielmino's *Self-Directed Learning Readiness Scale* (SDLRS). Nine major variable categories were found to be related to self-direction in learning as measured by the SDLRS over the last 12 years that preceded their investigation. Three of these were found to have statistically significant correlations (= .05): age ($r = -.549$), gender ($r = .636$), and dependence ($r = -.886$).

Gordon Eisenman, in "Self-Directed Learning — A Growth Process?" tested three hypotheses. The first hypothesis stated that parents' self-directed learning readiness (as measured by Guglielmino's SDLRS) would be related to their children's self-directed learning readiness (as measured by the E [elementary] version of the SDLRS). The second hypothesis stated that the teachers' self-directed learning readiness (SDLRS) would be related to the children's self-directed learning readiness (SDLRS-E). The third hypothesis stated that the children's cognitive abilities (as measured by the cognitive abilities test) would be related to their self-directed learning readiness (SDLRS-E). No statistically significant relationships were found.

Russell F. West and Ernest L. Bentley, Jr., in "Structural Analysis of the *Self-Directed Learning Readiness Scale:* A Confirmatory Factor Analysis Using LISREL Modeling," carried out a confirmatory factor analysis using the Linear Structural Relations Model (LISREL). Their results show that a six-factor model rather than the original eight-factor model best represents the underlying self-directed learning construct. Furthermore, according to these authors' conclusions, the overall SDLRS score seems to provide a more adequate measure than the highly correlated factor scores.

A Critical Synthesis of the Original Work

A detailed, critical synthesis of the entire original work has led to the identification of various themes. The purpose of the present study is to point out those themes that are considered to be most relevant to the specific concerns of continuing adult education practitioners.

The first section of the present study deals with general notions that are related to the conceptualization of the self-directed learning phenomenon. The second section deals with specific notions that are related to the practice of self-directed learning in formal as well as in informal educational settings.

Conceptual Issues

With regard to the conceptualization of the self-directed learning phenomenon, three distinct features stand out: its powers of attraction, its complexity, and its ambiguity.

The Concept's Powers of Attraction

Since the mid 1960s, adult self-directed learning has become a central concept in the field of adult education (Candy; Eisenman; Gerstner; West & Bentley). Various combined contextual, pedagogical, and ideological factors have contributed to increase this concept's powers of attraction. On the one hand, the formal system of education seems to have become incompatible with most of the needs and life situations of an increasingly large number of adults (Adekanmbi), especially with regard to the rapidly changing demands of the workplace (Candy). On the other hand, an increasing number of adult education practitioners as well as researchers — even from different ideological backgrounds — have advocated self-direction in learning (Candy; Gerstner; Jarvis). The formal pedagogical status quo has been questioned, while non traditional, alternative — and often self-directed — educational practices have been put forward (Adekanmbi).

The Concept's Complexity

The concept of self-directed learning already constitutes an important part of the field of adult education's knowledge base (Eisenman) and it is expected to continue to be a major, unifying concept (Eisenman; Gerstner) within this disparate area of research and practice. Yet, this concept's very definition is influenced by various different and often contradictory schools of thought (Gerstner) and frameworks.

Four Philosophical Perspectives

Self-directed learning has mostly been defined from four major philosophical perspectives: progressivist, humanist, behaviorist, and critical (Gerstner).

Progressivism, based on its faith in democracy and education, has had a strong impact on the whole North American adult education movement. Lindeman's (1926) emphasis on democracy and Dewey's (1938) emphasis on the individual's experience and self-direction well characterize this perspective (Gerstner).

Humanism, influenced by phenomenology, existentialism, and pragmatism, has greatly influenced, from the 1960s and 1970s until now, the optimistic, affirmative way of defining the individual learner. Maslow's (1970) emphasis on the person's innate striving for self-actualization and Rogers' (1961) emphasis on personal growth and autonomy well characterize this perspective. Knowles' (1973) basic assumptions regarding the adult learner correspond to this humanistic, philosophical perspective (Gerstner).

Behaviorism, influenced by the physical sciences' theoretical and methodological approach, has also exerted a strong influence on our understanding of self-directed learning. Bandura's (1977) social learning theory emphasizes the development of basic functions and skills by means of external incentives, in order to help the learner achieve self-direction and self-management. His theory well characterizes the current neo-behaviorist perspective (Gerstner).

The *critical* perspective is much more heterogeneous than the other three perspectives. It criticizes, from an antagonistic viewpoint, various social and intellectual systems' values and structures and is based on the belief that individuals can control and transform their own sociopolitical and personal environments. It is composed of three main approaches. The anarchist approach emphasizes the individual's autonomy with regard to the existing social systems (Gerstner). Illich represents this perspective. The Marxist approach focuses on the individual's empowerment and consequent social action. Freire's (1970) neo-Marxist approach, centered on the process of "conscientization," represents this perspective (Gerstner). The Freudian Left opposes the oppressive structures and roles imposed on the individual by the family, religion, and education. Mezirow's (1971) instrumental, dialogic, and self-reflective functions of adult learning correspond to this perspective (Gerstner). Brookfield's (1988) critical analysis of adult education and of self-directed learning in particular seems to correspond to both the neo-Marxist and the Freudian Left approaches (Gerstner).

Two Frameworks Centered on the Practice of Self-Directed Learning

Two specific descriptive and explanatory frameworks have been proposed in relation to the practice of adult self-directed learning as such. One is based on critical thinking, the other on practical thinking.

The proposed *critical thinking* framework rests upon Argyris' action science paradigm (Dorsey, et al). Within this framework, which is strongly influenced by Mezirow's Freudian Left perspective, adult educators are expected to increase the adult self-directed learners' critical reflection by offering them alternative frames of reference that should challenge their beliefs and assumptions (Dorsey, et al).

The proposed *practical thinking* framework rests mostly upon Vygotsky's activity theory as well as on concepts of practical problem solving (Peters). This new approach is linked to the self-directed learning overall approach: Embedded into everyday life and job-related situations, both practical problem solving and self-directed learning differ from the prevailing formal models of problem solving and formal models of instruction. Both focus on the adult's own strategies with regard to making decisions and with regard to taking action (Peters).

The Concept's Ambiguity

The concept of self-directed learning still remains ambiguous (Candy; Long) and ill-defined (Candy; Eisenman; Jarvis). The most important confusion regarding this catch-all notion (Jarvis) is related to its very nature (Candy): Some adult educators and researchers consider self-directed learning as a goal (Candy) that is related to the intrinsic personal capacity of the individual learner to be or to become autonomous (Candy; Gerstner). They consequently focus on the individual's personal development and personality characteristics (Long) and mostly value self-knowledge (Gerstner). Others rather consider self-directed learning as a process (Candy; Long) that is mostly related to extrinsic aspects of learning and self-instructional procedures. They consequently focus on learning and teaching strategies and mostly value instrumental knowledge, that is, information and skills leading to self-control and self-management (Gerstner).

Any basic definition focusing on self-directed learning as a process or method should take into account two major underlying notions: One has to do with the ownership of the self-directed learning endeavor, the other with the assistance sought in particular settings (Candy).

The degree of *ownership* may range on a continuum from a learner's total personal control and responsibility to his/her total reliance on institutionally controlled learning programs and structures (Adekanmbi; Candy; Long). A personally sponsored learning activity connotes a personal ownership of this activity (Long), while an institutionally sponsored learning activity connotes a social ownership of this same activity (Long).

The level of *assistance* sought by the adult learner may also range on a continuum from a total absence of institutional affiliation and support, given the learner's informal and independent educational setting, to a total formal, institutional affiliation and support, given the learner's formally structured educational setting (Candy; Long).

Practical Issues

Three major practical issues stand out: The dynamics of the self-directed learning process, the teacher-learner transaction, and the individual self-directed learner.

The Dynamics of the Self-Directed Learning Process

Practitioners and researchers too often assume that the self-directed learning process is similar to the formal instructional process (Nolan). They therefore focus on pre-established planning, goal setting, sequences, methods, and resources that correspond to formal instructional models (Cavaliere; Nolan). The natural self-directed learning process, however, does not seem to correspond to such a relatively static description of its nature. On the contrary, this dynamic learning process rather appears to be activated by the autonomous adult learner's self-monitored, contextual, and often fortuitous decisions and actions (Cavaliere; Nolan; Peters).

In order to foster self-directed learning with regard to institutionally sponsored learning activities (Long), it is important not to impose linear, prestructured learning activities. Negotiation becomes a key concept within this context (Jarvis). However, a learner-directed instructional process is not always appropriate. The use of learning contract projects, for example (Jarvis), may sometimes prove to be counterproductive, given the fact that learners must often master the basic notions of a structured learning content through dependent learning modalities before deciding to use more independent learning modalities (monitor theory) (Nolan).

The self-directed learning process seems to be characterized by various non-linear, cyclical stages that are related to the learner's inquiring, experimenting, theorizing, and actualizing (Cavaliere). All of these stages consist of basic cognitive processes (Cavaliere) that in turn require specific process skills (Long & Agyekum).

Process Skills

Process skills are considered to be essential to the learners' integration of the learning content and to their selection of efficient instructional and emotional support.

In the present continuing professional education context, agents are faced with the urgent need to foster the development of essential process skills. Only such skills will allow employees and professionals to be or continue to be proactive and self-directed with regard to gaining access to relevant knowledge (Long & Agyekum), selecting appropriate strategies (Peters), and assessing rapidly changing practice needs and requirements.

Critical thinking is one of the various essential self-directed learning skills (Eisenman). It is too often only related to Freire's neo-Marxist conscientization approach or to Mezirow's Freudian Left perspective transformation approach. These critical approaches are not only centered on the adult's learning process abilities and skills. They are also centered on the transmission of an implicit — sometimes explicit — learning content. Educators, within this ideological context, are often expected to provide alternative ideological frames of reference that advocate the modification of social or intellectual systems (Dorsey, et al; Gerstner).

Triggering Mechanism

The triggering mechanism of the complex learning stages or episodes (Cavaliere) may be self-induced or other-induced (Jarvis). It may even be teacher-initiated (Jarvis) within a formally structured environment. This mechanism is often activated by an immediate problem-solving situation or context (Cavaliere).

Self-Directed Learning Patterns

The adult learners' patterns may vary according to the type of knowledge or information they seek to acquire (Cavaliere; Sgroi); according to the formal, informal, and/or casual methods they select (Long & Agyekum); and according to the type of feedback they get from their learning environment and resources (Cavaliere). Informal information networks are proving to be most useful (Cavaliere).

Assessment and Feedback

In formal as well as in informal educational settings, many self-directed learners tend to assess their own progress frequently (Cavaliere), according to their needs, their aims, and their integration of the learning content (Jarvis). They do so by means of objective criteria based, for example, on the feedback of an expert and by means of subjective criteria based on their own constant and critical self-evaluation (Cavaliere).

In a structured educational environment, educators should help the adult learners with the evaluation of both their progress and their process (Adekanmbi). Furthermore, a process-centered, formative evaluation during the learning activities seems to be as important as the usual product-centered, summative evaluation at the end of these activities (Adekanmbi; Jarvis).

With regard to feedback in a formal environment, the teacher's or educator's frequent corrections and comments (turn-around-time) regarding the adult learners' progress seems to sustain these learners' motivation and commitment to learning (Adekanmbi). Feedback, in fact, seems to have more impact on the learners' motivation and choice of adequate learning strategies than it has on their cognitive processes (Cavaliere).

The Teacher-Learner Transaction

Any type of learning — including self-directed learning in natural settings as well as the various forms of assisted autodidaxy in formal educational settings (Sgroi) — is carried out in the context of interpersonal relationships between the learner and his/her teacher or facilitator (Adekanmbi; Candy). The quality of this relationship, which includes interpersonal contacts as well as instructional aspects (Candy), seems to be vital (Adekanmbi; Sgroi).

A Tension between Autonomy and Dependence

In a formally structured educational environment, this interactive and interdependent relationship is often characterized by the adult learners' cognitive and emotional resistance to their dependency on the teacher or expert who structures and organizes their learning activities (Nolan). Indeed, at nearly every stage of the learning process, this tension may arise between autonomy and dependence (Nolan), between control and deference (Sgroi).

The Adult Learners' Point of View

The adult learners' own perception of the assistance and direction they expect will have a direct impact on their relationship with their teacher/facilitator (Candy). For example, in formal settings, adult learners may have clear expectations with regard to their teacher's guidance (Sgroi). Given the adult learners' past learning experiences and specific expectations, some may find a particular form of assistance most adequate, while others may find this very same form totally inadequate and unacceptable (Candy).

In formal settings also, even when some adult learners temporarily adapt their self-teaching styles to match their teacher's style, they nevertheless still see themselves as autonomous individuals who remain in control of their own learning endeavor (Sgroi).

The Teacher's Point of View

The teacher or facilitator's view of learner autonomy will also impact directly on the teaching-learning transaction (Candy).

In a formal setting, for example, educational agents who value self-directedness in learning will more readily set teaching conditions that focus on the adults' active orientation to learning (Long) and apply instructional strategies that tend to develop self-directed learning abilities (Long).

However, educators should not assume that all adult learners prefer to be self-directed. In fact, many tend to choose structured, teacher-directed contexts (Jarvis).

Educators should not assume either that their use of formal instructional strategies that are centered on the development of the adult learners' self-directedness in learning (defined as a process) will necessarily lead to the development of the learners' personal autonomy (defined as a goal) (Candy).

The Individual Self-Directed Learner

Within the prevailing holistic approach, the adult's various intrinsic dimensions as a learner, as a person, and as an expert are considered to be dynamically related to corresponding extrinsic, self-directed learning processes and factors (Long & Agyekum). Within this approach, the adult learner's self-directed formal, informal, and fortuitous learning activities must be understood from his/her whole life perspective (Lambert & Rountree-Wyly; Sgroi).

Educational programs could become more and more tailored to suit each individual's interests, talents, and goals with regard to his/her career or work-related personal development.

A Subjective Viewpoint

Most dimensions relating to self-directed learners have been studied from a subjective perspective, that is, from the individual learner's own perceptions and interpretations. This subjective frame of reference is most important, given the fact that it will indeed influence the learners' strategies, the kinds of assistance they expect and even their learning outcomes (Candy). The main subjective elements are the following:

1.   The adult learners' beliefs, wants, intentions, and purposes seem to guide most of their decisions and actions (Peters). Many adult learners also seem to be strongly driven toward personal accomplishment or recognition (Long & Agyekum).
2.   The adult learners' myths or convictions based on their past learning experiences may promote or hinder their learning endeavor (Candy).
3.   In formal as well as in informal educational settings, the adults' references to their prior knowledge may also help or hinder their acquisition and application of new knowledge. The adults' relevant prior knowledge may allow further integration of the new knowledge, while erroneous or misinformed preconceptions may impede their ongoing learning and instructional processes (Candy).
4.   The study of the adults' self-directed learning readiness related to specific learning skills and attitudes may contribute to diagnose their potential for self-directedness in learning (Eisenman; West & Bentley). As defined here, this specific notion is measured by L. M. Guglielmino's *Self-Directed Learning Readiness*

Scale (SDLRS) (1977) (Eisenman; McCune, Guglielmino & Garcia; West & Bentley).

5. Some specific personality dimensions related to the adult learners' initiative and persistence may contribute to explain these adults' proactive, continuing learning approaches (Eisenman). Some of these personality dimensions have been identified by L. F. Oddi's *Oddi Continuing Learning Inventory* (OCLI) (1984) (Eisenman).

An Objective Viewpoint

Very few dimensions relating to individual, continuing, self-directed learners have been studied from an objective perspective, that is, from external observers' perceptions and measurements.

1. For example, the possible relationship between the self-directed learning process and the adult learners' cognitive abilities has not been studied satisfactorily yet (Eisenman).
2. Self-instructional process skills — such as critical thinking — have not been studied satisfactorily yet (Eisenman).

Conclusion

In order to adapt to increasingly numerous and complex demands of competency and flexibility in the work place, continuing, professional, training practitioners and managers might have to revise some of their instructional approaches and assumptions.

The actual shift in our definitions of what is or what should be efficient and meaningful learning seems to be mostly evident in the self-directed learning field of practice and research. As we have seen throughout this chapter, this relatively new field of interest seems indeed to offer new perspectives that may prove to be most relevant to the design, delivery, and evaluation of continuing adult education in the workplace. The field of self-directed learning questions the pedagogical status quo and proposes alternative educational practices that could be more compatible with the adult learners' needs and expectations. It is studied from various ideological viewpoints. It focuses on the adult learners' ownership of the learning endeavor, on the dynamics of a natural, non-linear learning process, and on teacher-learner transactions. Finally, it puts forward a holistic approach to the individual learners' multifaceted reality.

References

Bandura, A. (1977). *Social learning theory.* Englewood Cliffs, NJ: Prentice Hall.

Brookfield, S. D. (1988). Conceptual, methodological and practical ambiguities in self-directed learning. In H. B. Long & Associates, *Self-directed learning: Application and theory.* Athens, GA: Adult Education Department, University of Georgia.

Dewey, J. (1938). *Experience and education.* NY: Macmillan.

Freire, P. (1970). *Pedagogy of the oppressed.* NY: Herder and Herder.

Guglielmino, L. M. (1977). Development of the self-directed learning readiness scale. (Doctoral dissertation, University of Georgia). *Dissertation Abstracts International, 38,* 6467A.

Long, H. B. and Associates. (1990). *Advances in research and practice in self-directed learning.* Norman, OK: Oklahoma Research Center for Continuing Professional and Higher Education of the University of Oklahoma.

Knowles, M. S. (1973). *The adult learner: A neglected species* (2nd ed.). Houston, TX: Gulf Publishing.

Lindeman, E. C. (1926). *The meaning of adult education.* NY: New Republic.

Maslow, A. H. (1970). *Motivation and personality.* NY: Harper and Row.

Mezirow, J. (1971). Toward a theory of practice. *Adult Education Journal, 21,* 135-147.

Oddi, L. F. (1984). Development of an instrument to measure self-directed continuing learning. (Doctoral dissertation, Northern Illinois University.) *Dissertation Abstracts International, 46,* 49A.

Rogers, C. R. (1961). *On becoming a person: A therapist's view of psychotherapy.* Boston, MA: Houghton, Mifflin.

Notes